Cities

created by John McGreevy

Clarkson N. Potter, Inc./Publishers NEW YORK

DISTRIBUTED BY CROWN PUBLISHERS, INC.

Inquiries should be addressed to Clarkson N. Potter,
Inc., One Park Avenue, New York, New York 10016

Printed in Canada

Published simultaneously in Canada by
Lester & Orpen Dennys Ltd.

LIBRARY OF CONGRESS CATALOGING IN PUBLICATION DATA
Main entry under title:

Cities.

   1. Cities and towns. I. McGreevy, John.
HT151.C568   1981   307.7′6   81-287
ISBN 0-517-544695   AACR1

10 9 8 7 6 5 4 3 2 1
First edition

Contents

Introduction

Cities, in their infinite variety, express the complexity and intensity of the human experience. Nowhere do you find the tragedy and comedy of daily life more vividly enacted than in the great metropolitan areas of the world.

I have always been a lover of cities, finding in the passing parade on any street corner an inexhaustible source for reflection on the way we live. So, the chance of visiting some of the great cities of the world in the company of gifted and highly articulate human beings was an opportunity not to be missed.

Here are thirteen impressions of world cities as seen through the eyes of people intimately connected to them. You will not find balance or objectivity here. Rather, the points of view expressed are deeply personal, some of them deriving from memories of experiences and passions that make up a person's origins and others from a sense of triumph over those origins. Whether it is Chicago, exuberantly presented in Studs Terkel's quest for beauty, Jerusalem captured in Elie Wiesel's psalm to history, or the Rome of Anthony Burgess in all its paganism, the unifying link is the feeling of uniqueness projected by each one for his particular city.

This book was three years in the making. We started in Glasgow with R. D. Laing and ended in Athens, the first of the great cities, with Melina Mercouri. Our aim throughout was to present spontaneous portraits of some of the world's remarkable places. Thus, to a large extent, we arrived in each city without preconceived ideas, but attempted to capture immediate reactions to events and places as we came upon them. This improvisational approach afforded us many more opportunities for spontaneity than a more formal one would have permitted.

While we appeared to be engaged in a series of guided tours, I confess that, more often than not, I looked forward to the possibility of capturing those accidental moments of personal idiosyncrasy that express the spirit of our hosts. Peter Ustinov, for example, moving through the rush hour crowds of Leningrad with considerable *sang-froid*, seemingly talking to himself and receiving astonished looks from the passers-by; Jonathan Miller invoking the spirit of his dead nanny in Highgate Cemetery; Glenn Gould singing Mahler *lieder* at dawn to the elephants in Toronto's zoo, such moments revealing as much about the person as about the city.

It required considerable courage on my guests' part to improvise their way through each city and trust that what would eventually emerge would be coherent and express something personal. While most of what you read was created for the spoken rather than the written word, it captures very well the essential wit and humanity of our hosts.

No venture such as this is achieved without the generous assistance of a great number of people. In each of the cities we visited we were met with the greatest cordiality and co-operation. Many officials associated with city and government departments extended themselves without hesitation and to them go both a deep sigh of relief and a sincere expression of gratitude. A special acknowledgment goes to Eve Orpen who had the original idea for this book. Alas, she did not live to see its publication.

Ultimately, my deepest gratitude must go to the thirteen remarkable people who contributed most to this book. They have enriched my life immeasurably, as they are about to enrich yours.

John McGreevy
Toronto, Christmas 1980

Cities

PETER USTINOV'S
Leningrad

PETER USTINOV'S
Leningrad

City of Peter the Great, city of Lenin, and birthplace of the Russian Revolution. I wasn't born here, but my parents met and married here before moving to London, where I was born. I have it on the best authority that I was conceived here, and you can't get much closer emotionally to a city than that. I must say that I love Leningrad.

Opposite page   Pushkin Memorial

Venice, Russians say jokingly, is the
Leningrad of the south. But,
perhaps, Leningrad is the Amsterdam
of the east. Like Amsterdam,
Leningrad is essentially a maritime
city. Nobody is ever far from the
water or the early morning mist.
Sixty-eight rivers and canals divide
the land on which Leningrad is built,
and there are nearly four hundred
bridges in different parts of the town.

The larger bridges—of which there are nine—are across the River Neva, and are raised between two and three o'clock in the morning during the navigable months to allow the passage of ships. Neva, which sounds so romantic, is in fact the Finnish word for mud.

Founded in 1703 by Peter the Great, the city was initially named St. Petersburg, was renamed Petrograd in 1914, and finally became Leningrad in 1924. Peter's obsession was with the sea. He saw in the city an absolutely critical location that gave access to the Baltic. He took a calculated risk in locating his capital here. It stands on the most unpromising marshlands and is still prone to very serious flooding despite the system of canals he built to control the water.

Peter was, by any standards, an extraordinary man. Six foot eight inches tall, he bestrode the countryside like a colossus, with ideas on everything and, evidently, with a great sense of fun and humour. He created the first museum of the Russian people here; and in order to induce people to visit it, he tempted them with a glass of vodka at the gate —a highly original idea which is the mark of his visionary genius about the most unexpected things.

Peter died of pneumonia in 1725 at the age of fifty-three, and asked to be buried in the church of the Fortress of Peter and Paul, where he now lies surrounded by his loved ones —his second wife, Catherine I, and his favourite daughter, Elizabeth.

Opposite page   The River Neva
Above   The Fortress of Peter and Paul

Along the quayside of the Griboyedov Canal, which was named for one of Russia's greatest satirists, the novelist Dostoyevsky used to brood and meditate during the long white nights when it was hard to sleep but easy to think dark thoughts. It was on this quayside that an event took place worthy of Dostoyevsky's pen. It happened just after the great writer had died in 1881.

The autocratic Czar Alexander II was driving in his carriage along the bank, from Nevsky Prospekt to the Winter Palace, when two terrorist bombs exploded. The czar's legs were blown off and subsequently he died. The leader of the conspiracy, Zhelyabov, was already in prison, having been arrested two days previously, but his mistress, Sophia Perovskaya, daughter of a former governor of the city, brilliantly and cold-bloodedly carried on with the plot, only to be arrested later. Nicholas II built the Church of the Spilled Blood on the spot to commemorate this sorry event. The conspirators, five of them, were hanged in the last public execution in Czarist Russia.

It is curious that previously Dostoyevsky had also been accused of conspiracy. He was about to be shot when an officer galloped in with a pardon, an event carefully prepared in advance, of course. Dostoyevsky was sent to Siberia for five years, and then spent another five years as a private in the army. Thank heavens his broodings beside the Griboyedov Canal became public, because they led to *Crime and Punishment*, *The Brothers Karamazov*, *The Possessed*, and other masterpieces.

Griboyedov Canal

St. Isaac's Cathedral is the third
largest domed building in Europe,
after St. Peter's in Rome and St.
Paul's in London, and it appears
heavier than either of those two. It is
a typical example of mid-nineteenth-
century megalomania. Apparently the
gilding of the dome cost sixty
thousand people their lives, all dying
of mercury poisoning. In these terms,
it threatens the records of the
pyramids of ancient Egypt, and it
stands as a monument to wealth as
well as to beauty.

The Cathedral was finished in
1858, having taken forty years to
build, half a lifetime. Montferrand,
the designer, regarded it as his life's
work and promptly died two months
after it was completed. The painters
Bryulov and Bruni, who contributed
most to its interior decoration, died
during the construction.

St. Isaac's was the place intended
for royal baptisms, marriages, and the
like. It is also known as a museum of
minerals because it includes many of
the rarest semiprecious stones. The
large columns are of malachite, the
smaller ones of lapis lazuli and these
surround a stained-glass window produced by masters from Munich,
Germany. The saints near the altar
are depicted in a magnificently
luminous Russian mosaic technique,
and they all have some connection by
name or otherwise with the royal
family — including St. Isaac, whose
name day happened to coincide with
Peter the Great's birthday.

Mysteriously, St. Isaac stands with
the plans of this very cathedral in his

hand, looking skyward for celestial
approval.

The acoustics of the building are
extraordinary because of the Russian
technique of building the cupolas out
of empty clay pots which are very
light and resonant. Fourteen thousand worshippers could stand or, if
they were seized by a special surge of
devotion or fatigue, kneel, but they
could not sit. Only the czar and his
family could sit. However devoted
they became, the royal family had no
need to kneel—confirmation of the
czar's high standing with the true god.

Opposite page   Interior of St. Isaac's
                                 Cathedral
Above   The painting of St. Isaac

Smolny Cathedral

Leningrad, at its beginning, was as much a
magnet to artists as Hollywood has been to
film-makers. Many people came here to make
their fortunes because they knew their talents
would be needed for such a bold conception.
And so it was that a great number of foreign
architects joined their Russian counterparts in
the building of the capital.

The Smolny Cathedral was built by
Rastrelli, probably the most famous of all
Leningrad's architects, for Elizabeth, daughter
of Peter the Great. Rastrelli was an Italian who
became very Russian, synthesizing the Italian
baroque with the Russian traditional style, an
easily recognizable and quite beautiful marriage. The cathedral is a very impressive
building crowned by those very Russian

symbols, a central onion-shaped cupola representing God, with four smaller cupolas around it, standing for the Apostles — Matthew, Mark, Luke, and John.

Rastrelli was supposed to have been in love with Elizabeth, and therefore his cathedral is blue to conform with the blueness of her eyes. Yet some experts say her eyes were green. This is the kind of insoluble dispute that ends friendship between experts.

Amid the baleful and raucous noise of the northern crows, Rastrelli also built a palatial country retreat for Elizabeth, with the same tribute to the colour of her eyes. She didn't live very long to enjoy it and was succeeded by Catherine the Great, an impoverished German princess who really had no claim to the throne, but got it all the same.

Rastrelli's retreat for Elizabeth

Paul I's palace at Pavlovsk

Catherine the Great had many children from undisclosed sources, including Czar Paul I who was to be her successor, but for whom she did not care. She lived with her two grandsons, nurturing them and hoping that they would become czars, one of Russia and the other of Byzantium, because she cherished the idea that this ancient dual empire would be revived under the aegis of Russia.

So much did she dislike her son Paul that she ostracized him from her great palace and built him a more beautiful palace at Pavlovsk,

Statue of Paul I

designed by the Scottish architect Charles Cameron. Paul was a very difficult character, and many thought him mad. He used to belabour troops on the parade ground and play with tin soldiers in bed.

I happen to know a great deal about Paul I because my own great-great-great-grandfather came to the Russian capital from France, just after the French Revolution, to become Master of the Royal Mouth—in other words, he was in charge of the royal kitchens; however you describe it, it was no easy job. He married the royal midwife, Fräulein Grope, and between them, in spite of these difficult circumstances, they had enough sense of humour to have twenty-three children, most of whom survived—unlike Czar Paul, who was murdered by his own bodyguard.

Leningrad is a city of magnificent proportions. Rossi Street, named after the Italian architect who built it at the beginning of the nineteenth century, is claimed to be the most elegant street in the city, but of course it is not a street in the normal sense of the word. There are no shops, and very little traffic. It is an exercise in the architectural skill of the period. It is exactly twenty-one metres across and the buildings are twenty-one metres high. The terraced buildings on either side are exactly two hundred and ten metres long, ten times twenty-one metres.

At the far end of Rossi Street is the Pushkin Theatre, formerly the Alexandrinsky Theatre for Dramatic Art, for which Ostrovsky wrote several plays. On the left is a dance museum, and on the right the famous Kirov dance school, associated with such illustrious pupils as Nijinsky, Karsavina, and Pavlova. The street is a jewel worthy of Leningrad. Bravo, Rossi!

Pushkin Theatre

The Hermitage Museum, one of the world's great galleries, contains over two and one-half million paintings and objets d'art strewn on more than fifty thousand square metres of wall in three hundred and seventy-four rooms. A visitor avid to see it all must start very early and be prepared for a walk of just under fifteen miles, punctuated inevitably by pauses before the innumerable masterpieces. It stands to reason that even Americans have found it difficult to do in a day, and Russians have found it as difficult to do in a lifetime.

In the heart of bustling Leningrad there is a small island of peace and quiet called the Lavra — a Russian Poets' Corner, where most of the country's great artists are laid to rest. The mighty five of Russian music are buried here:

Rimsky-Korsakov, Borodin, Mussorgsky,
César Cui, and Balakirev. And right next to
them, Tchaikovsky. All the old battles are now
forgotten. They lie here in peace. Dostoyevsky
is in another part of this little dell. And I am
glad to have found that my own great-
great-grandfather, whose name was Cavos and
who came from Venice to conduct in the
Imperial theatres, is lying between
Bortniansky, one of the founders of Russian
church music, and Dargomijsky, one of the
most interesting composers Russia has produced.

Opposite page   Hermitage Museum
Below, this page   The Lavra

Lenin Square lies in front of the Finland Station. It was here that Vladimir Ilyich Lenin returned on April 17, 1917, after ten years of exile. His reputation had so grown during his absence that an enormous crowd was on hand to greet him. He made that famous speech of his in the square, saying that a socialist revolution was possible in Russia. "Now or never," he urged, and the rest is history. Lenin was the only man with enough strength and charisma to wrest the name of the city from Peter the Great, and eventually it became Leningrad. Both he and Peter the Great continue to cast their lights over this splendid city.

On November 10, 1917, Lenin occupied the Smolny Institute, a fashionable establishment where the daughters of the aristocracy learned table manners and other forms of etiquette. (The daughters of the nobility are, of course, no longer there; their descendants are dispersed all over the world doing useful jobs.) Lenin ran the government from the Institute. His rooms show an austerity that would have put even Peter the Great to shame. But then Lenin lived in more austere times. The war was still on and Leningrad was the real nerve centre of a fledgling regime trying to find peace and to begin the construction of a new form of society. In 1918 the capital was moved to Moscow.

Lenin Square

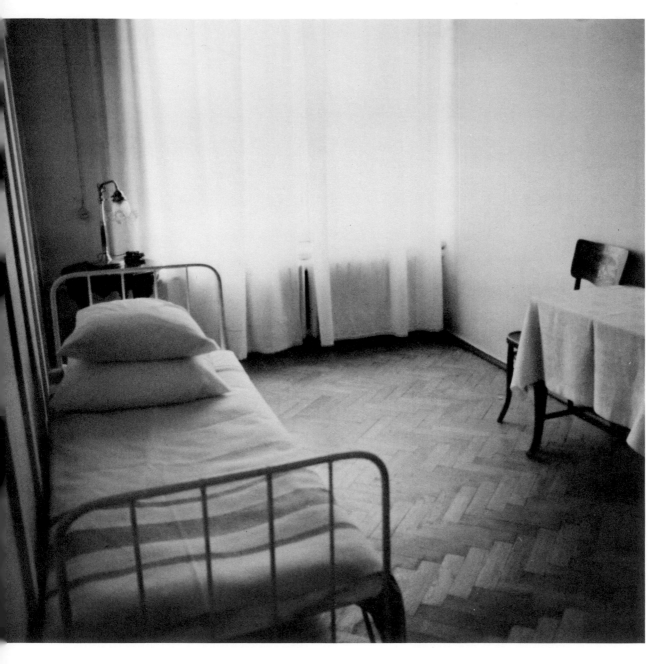

Lenin's quarters at the Smolny Institute

Memorial at Piskarevsky

On June 22, 1941, the Russians were attacked by Hitler, and within two months the Germans were hammering at the gates of Leningrad. They advanced to within six miles of the centre of the city. Nine hundred days the siege lasted, one of the longest and most dramatic in the history of warfare. The sacrifices of these dour and modest people were tremendous and unspoken. At the village of Piskarevsky, on the outskirts of the city, between 400,000 and 600,000 lie buried in a communal grave. People had no energy to dig, and so the bodies were left in the streets and eventually were gathered together for burial when spring had softened the earth. Altogether, over a million people died in this city, resisting the German invaders. But the Germans never managed to capture it.

At Piskarevsky, as elsewhere in Russia, flowers are left anonymously —flowers for the nameless people who died in defence of their great city. The memorial is now a place of repose, a place of enormous power and dignity, and a flame burns eternally there as it should.

City of Peter, city of Lenin, city of nearly four and one-half million people who are still mourning a million dead: people who seem sometimes reserved, standoffish, even surly, and at other times playful, mischievous, and full of fun. These are the manifestations of a great timidity, almost demureness, and a sense of what is right and wrong, what is to be done and what is not to be done. All this disguises an inherent humanity and an inherent toughness.

In Leningrad, there are faces of emancipation, women with responsible and dignified professions and men with purpose in their walk. There are dreamers and idlers, inquisitive people, and people with faces closed on their thoughts. And among the faces of the old, there are impervious expressions insensitive to change, seeing all times as more or less hard, grateful for the momentary clemency of the weather and the absence of war. These are the men and women of Leningrad, the triumph of whose lives is not opulence or frivolity, but survival, and the infinite luxury of still being alive.

ELIE WIESEL'S
Jerusalem

ELIE WIESEL'S
Jerusalem

There is something strange about Jerusalem, something unique about it. When I visited the city for the first time, I had a feeling that it was not the first time, that I had been here many times before. But now each time I come back to Jerusalem, I have a feeling that it is my first time here.

The Lions' Gate

One enters Jerusalem as one enters a dream—breathless. A dream filled with anguish, joy, wonder and, above all, beauty. A dream filled with colours, images, memories. A dream filled with your own past, a past as rich as the past of mankind. This city, symbolically but ironically called the City of Peace, has invited so many invaders, so many conquerors who didn't want to conquer: the Byzantines, the Turks, the Mamelukes, the Arabs, and the Crusaders. And now the City of Peace has come into its own again, has reconquered its past, and we are all part of it.

You enter through one of its gates into streets and alleys filled with sunshine and shadows; you cut through crowds of merchants and worshippers, and you look at them and at yourself as though you all belonged to another era: a walk in this eternal city leads you back in time, back to a child's spellbound and spellbinding city where all are mysterious sages and princes.

I remember it all: legends and promises, prayers and benedictions, long ago and next year. David and the Messiah. Exile and homecoming. What would I be, as a Jew, without this city, the most Jewish city and the most universal as well?

All my memories are linked to its memories. The laws. The rituals. The Temple. The priests. The prophets. The catastrophe. The surviving stones.

This magnificent dome, extraordinary in its grace and beauty, is holy to both Jews and Moslems. It is called the Temple Mount, and here the first and second Temples of Israel were built. But here also the Moslems, when they drove the Byzantine forces from Jerusalem in the seventh century, built the Dome on the Rock, a shrine on the basic foundation of the world.

There are many legends attached to this place, as there are to any building, any stone, any shadow, any tree in this city. Legend has it that Mohammed the Prophet flew from here when he ascended to heaven. And that Abraham prayed here, and Solomon prayed here, and David and Elijah and, of course, Mohammed himself. And furthermore, legend has it that, when Cain and Abel quarrelled and fought and one killed the other, it was here that the struggle took place.

This is probably the holiest place in the entire world. Only once has it yielded to an alien power and religion—in the eleventh century the Crusaders took it and called it Templus Domini—but that didn't last for long. And this beautiful and extraordinary building has stood, almost unchanged, for some thirteen hundred years.

Temple Mount

The Wailing Wall

I remember my first discovery of the Wailing Wall. It was during the Six-Day War; the war was still on and we had just arrived at this spot. I remember moving my lips — and what I said then I have been saying ever since: I belong here, in this very place. . . . We all do. I recall the words: "Here I am, Elie Wiesel. . . ." And I remembered my father, my mother, my teachers, my friends. I said: ". . . and I am the eye that is looking at the eye that is looking. I shall look so hard that I shall go mad. So what? I shall sing, I shall sing, and I shall become blind. So what? I shall still remember. I shall dream, I shall dream my own dream, the dream of my people, which is the dream of mankind."

I had never felt what I felt here. Here at the wall you remember — here at the wall you cannot but remember — and I see before my eyes the kings and the prophets, the poets and the beggars, and all those Jews and non-Jews who, through all the centuries, were looking for some consolation, for some comfort, for some hope, and who would come here to speak about it.

Wherever you go in Jerusalem, down small streets, in dark corners, you stumble upon history. So many legions, so many commanders, so many enemies have invaded the city: Pompey, Titus and, earlier, Pontius Pilate. You remember those who defended the Temple and the city. You can still trace a tunnel cut through the rock by King Hezekiah to bring in water from outside during times of siege. In the surrounding hills you can hear echoes of Bar Kochba and his guerrillas preparing for war. You dig and you meet the Jewish past, for Byzantine churches are built over Jewish monuments.

Here a Jew feels more Jewish, and a Christian more Christian, since the city also encloses Christendom's holiest shrines. There is no place more sacred, more important, and more central for Christians than the Church of the Holy Sepulchre, over the spot where, according to tradition, the body of Jesus Christ rested before His ascent to heaven. And through the city runs the most sacred road in Christian history, the Via Dolorosa that Christ followed on His way to His crucifixion at Golgotha.

I am not a Christian, I cannot do more than speak of these things with respect. But here in Jerusalem, perhaps for the first time in two thousand years, all religions are respected by the faithful who share belief in the same God.

The Church of the Holy Sepulchre

Mea Shearim

Within the walls of Jerusalem, you are obsessed by history. No other city has such evocative power to bring the past back to life. Just walk, and listen. Someone is singing and you think of David. Someone is questioning and you think of Judah ha-Levi. Someone is conjuring the heavens in the name of hope and you think of Rabbi Akiba. Samuel and Isaiah, Elijah and Jeremiah. Hezekiah and his underground tunnels. The Herod Agrippas. Somehow they all invade your memory as it touches Jerusalem's.

Mea Shearim, a hundred years old, an enclave in Jerusalem and in time, reminds me of the Jerusalem of my childhood, because here people are still extremely religious, and whatever they do now, they have been doing for the last two thousand years. Because images are considered sacrilegious, it is often impossible to take photographs. When people see a camera, they run away or begin shouting or cover their faces.

The houses are exactly like those I knew as a child—small, poor, and clean—but the people are fervent. Everybody gets ready for the coming of the Sabbath: small children prepare their homes for Sabbath, mothers prepare their meals for Sabbath. Here, in a sense, is the Sabbath of Jerusalem. Some of these people do not recognize the authority of the State of Israel. Since the Messiah hasn't come yet, they maintain that there should be no state at all. However, they are a minority— and although they do not recognize us, we recognize them.

With rare and tragic interruptions, there have always been Jews in Jerusalem. Recent excavations have shown that the earliest settlers, dating back to the seventh century before the Christian era, were Jewish. However, some parts of the city are lucky, some are

not; and that part—now called the Jewish
quarter of the Old City—is not. Somehow it
has always suffered and endured all the
incursions and cruelties of the invaders. Under
Herod and during the Roman period, Jews
lived in what was called the Upper City. Later,
during the rebellion against the Romans,
against the legions of Titus, they fought in the
caves. During the Bar Kochba rebellion they
fought like lions on this very spot. And still
later, when they came from all the lands of
persecution, from Spain, from Portugal, fleeing
from the Inquisition, they settled here and
built synagogues with magic and ancient
names, full of wonder and piety. These were
all destroyed again and again, rebuilt again and
again. The last time was in 1948, when the
Jordanians destroyed the synagogues and the
entire Jewish quarter. I remember when we
came into this place in 1967 with the first
paratroopers. Many of the paratroopers wept
because they saw the sanctuaries in ruins. But
now they have all been reconstructed. There
are weddings being celebrated in the
synagogues; services are taking place every
day; sages come from faraway lands to see the
miracle of reconstruction, for this is the miracle
of Jerusalem: we can build upon ruins. When I
come here—and I love to come to this place—
it's because I remember that Jerusalem has
been destroyed seventeen times, and seventeen times reconstructed.

When you look around and see the caves and the walls, you realize that this is a city of height and a city of depth. Somehow, you feel more humble than ever here; and, at the same time, you feel prouder than ever. You feel humble because the city is older than you, because the city is richer than any human being can ever hope to become. At night, I can literally hear the footsteps of Hezekiah, the last king of the First Temple era, as he fled through the secret caves to escape the siege. I can hear the Babylonians as they took him prisoner. And I can hear the prophet Jeremiah as he lamented. You can hear all those sounds in the city; you can almost hear the silence that preceded them and the silence that came after.

In ancient times on Yom Kippur, the holiest day of the Jewish year, there was a watchman whose task it was to stand on the walls of Jerusalem and wait for the first light. When he caught a glimpse of that light, he would shout, "*Bacai! Bacai!*" — "The light has arrived." He saw the light and set in motion the process of all the things that were supposed to happen that day. We have seen that light sometimes in the morning, and often we have caught its refractions later in the day. But for us the light is usually expressed in words and we remember only the tales of that light, the tales of those days. Mostly these tales are sad tales, because what marked our imagination and our memory was the destruction of this city and its beauty. Except when you speak of the first light. The first light of Jerusalem contains so much beauty and so much hope that all you can do is try to take it into you and give it unto others. And therefore Jerusalem, for me, has been and is this light, not only for my people but for mankind.

Pagan temples are replacing synagogues. Churches are built upon synagogues. Monuments are erected over houses of prayer and study. Nevertheless, all attempts to tamper with the Jewish soul of the city have failed: throughout the centuries Jerusalem has remained the symbol of Jewish continuity and endurance. When Jews pray in other countries, they turn towards the Holy Land. When they pray within the Holy Land, they turn towards Jerusalem. No city is linked to so many customs, no city has inspired so many legends. Though afflicted and wounded, Jerusalem has outlived its enemies.

There is strength in this city's walls, there is power, there is beauty, and there is majesty. I wish I could say that they are two thousand or three thousand years old, but they are not. In fact, they were built, or rather rebuilt, by Suleiman the Magnificent in 1538. But here and there are to be found some remnants of the walls built by Herod Agrippa. The walls were important because Jerusalem, exposed to so many enemies and invaders, lacked natural protection. But somehow, the enemy always managed to get through, to destroy the city, the inhabitants, and the culture inside these walls.

The marketplace outside the walls is busiest in the morning hours. Before the daily wave of heat hits the outskirts of the city, tourists come to watch the Arabs and to trade and buy. Has this changed much since the days of Suleiman? But then, has anything changed here? Jerusalem changes and stays the same. It acquires new layers, but it does not give up the old. The old ways are often more important than the new, because the old ways remind us of beginnings, the Jewish beginnings in Jerusalem.

"Wherever I go," a great Jewish storyteller has said, "my steps lead me to Jerusalem." And as for me, I could say that whenever I speak, I

speak about Jerusalem. There is something about this city that cannot but move you — to smile, to weep, surely to remember. I knew its name before I knew my own. My first lullaby was about Jerusalem as were the first tales I heard and the first prayer I uttered. The Talmud says that if a man loses his way, in the desert or anywhere else, and does not know how or where to direct his prayers, he should concentrate his mind on Jerusalem. It is the centre, it is the bearing. Whenever I feel lost, I think of Jerusalem and feel stronger, know where to go, and sometimes what to say. There are very beautiful tales I remember, and some of them I try to weave into my songs and my tales. But what is Jerusalem if not the tale of my tales, the dream of my dreams? What is Jerusalem if not a memory much more than my own?

GEORGE PLIMPTON'S
New York

GEORGE PLIMPTON'S
New York

I don't suppose any city in the world has as bad a reputation or a press as New York City. Calcutta, perhaps. But with New York, everywhere you go, people wonder when the city's going to collapse from financial instability or when it's going to slide gracefully into the Atlantic Ocean. They want to know when it's going to burn itself out of existence.

The Brooklyn Bridge

Many of the people who have doubts about New York haven't been here, or if they have, they've shot through the city without really giving it a chance. That's too bad, because of all the marvels of man, New York deserves our attention, our study. Here is focused almost everything we should be proud of, and perhaps a little scared of, too: power, imagination, energy, competitiveness. It's a place where invariably even the extraordinary is commonplace.

Even this city's detractors can't come over one of these bridges and deposit themselves in Manhattan without feeling the energy of its pulse. It's maddening sometimes, exhilarating always, but it does take time to adjust to the pace. That is what unnerves people when they come here for the first time. That pace. Their eyes pop. They feel slightly dizzy. They don't know how people can relax at such a pace.

Ellis Island was the starting point for
many New Yorkers. A derelict ferry-
boat bears that same prosaic name
and was once the means by which
most new arrivals were carried over
from the immigration station on the
island to Manhattan. The ferry was
put into commission in 1904, did its
job for fifty years, and was then laid
up here; it finally succumbed to the
hurricane of 1968. It's one of the few
remaining artifacts on this island that
suggests what went on, the movement of millions into the United
States. The people from the regional
headquarters of the Department of
the Interior in Boston come down
every once in a while in the hope that
they can restore the boat. But
obviously the chances are very slim
and soon this relic of massive
immigration is going to disappear.

Ellis Island was the gateway. Some
sixteen million people passed through
the huge processing room of the
Immigration Department, a million
annually from Europe during the
great years of immigration early in
this century. The immigrants came in
steamships and liners that berthed
nearby on the Hudson River; then,
while the first- and second-class
passengers went ashore immediately,
the steerage people were brought to
the island by barge to be processed in
this vast room, a procedure that took
five hours. Then they were ferried
across to Manhattan to start their lives
again.

Ellis Island

Opposite page   The Ellis Island ferry

Today, there is a parade for almost
every ethnic community in the city.
Parades go on here all the time. Fifth
Avenue is the traditional parade
route. There's usually a green stripe
down the middle of it for St. Patrick's
Day. And there's a parade here on
Veterans' Day. And Puerto Rican
Day. The Columbus Day parade, the

Italian holiday, is one of the longest
parades. It goes on for hours and
hours.

I think it's fair to say that the New
York population is divided into two
parts: those who like to parade, and
those who like to watch parades, with
the edge going perhaps to the former.
They love to show off, a kind of
personal exuberance on display,
perhaps just to prove that they can
survive the honeycomb existence of
this city with considerable flair and
spirit.

Some of the immigrants must have
gone down and leaned over the
parapet of Ellis Island to look out at
the great towers of lower Manhattan,
possibly the most astonishing view in
the world. Of course the skyline has
changed a bit since those times. The
twin towers of the Trade Center
there, and some of those dark office
buildings, are new. But the sense of
the skyline was certainly there and
some of the immigrants gazing at it
must have been overtaken by fore-
boding at so much that was waiting to
be understood. For others, there
must have been a sense of anticipa-
tion, of excitement. But surely, for all
of them, a sense of adventure. You
can almost hear the echoes — Hello,
America. Hello, America. . . .

What became of them? Of course,
we were all immigrants at one time,
and through generations we became
assimilated into this city's life — the
melting pot, as it's called. But what is
important is that many brought with
them what they could have left
behind, their cultures, so that communities as distinctive as those of the
old country were established throughout the city. Little Italy. Chinatown.
The Germans of Yorkville. The
Slovak community in the East 70s.
The Puerto Ricans in East Harlem.
There is no city in the world that has
quite this astonishing mix of cultures.

And all of it very vital to New Yorkers as a defence against the dehumanization of the huge urban development.

With such density, there are problems, pickpockets, muggers, and there's a police force as large as an army. But violence is not as much a factor as New York's detractors insist. New York spends much more time on friendly arts and pastimes.

The Chrysler Building

Harlem used to be the centre of entertainment that Broadway still is. A landmark of Broadway is 45th Street, one of the most famous theatre boulevards in the world. A very distinctive place, because New York has a love affair with its theatre. It's a great tradition to get up and go to Broadway to relax after the traumas of the working day, to see what's going on in the world of the theatre.

Of course there are two sides to that world. On the other side of the footlights it's not a place to relax, it's enormously competitive, with everyone desperately trying to become a star, to get a name up in lights. Tammy Grimes, a friend of mine, started out as a young actress in Boston, but now her name is familiar

on the marquees of Broadway. Why Broadway?
"Well," she said, "New York is the heart, isn't
it? It's still considered the centre of the theatre.
When you're a kid and decide to become part
of this profession, not really knowing what the
profession is all about, you only think in terms
of coming to New York, to Broadway, that's
final, that's the peak. When you make it in
New York that means you've made it."

What marks off Central Park from the other great parks of the world, comparing it, say, with the Tivoli or Luxembourg Gardens, is the way it's used by New Yorkers. It's not much used in a socializing sense, for walks or to look at the scenery, but it is very heavily used for athletics. If you go to the park in this city, you almost automatically reach for a ball or put your feet into a pair of sneakers, because the park is largely taken up with playgrounds, baseball diamonds, football fields. You can see almost any type of athletic activity going on here. I've seen bicycle polo, for example: Argentinians thrashing round on little bicycles with polo sticks. I've seen croquet played here. People fly kites. I've even seen a man with a niblick and golf balls. Bicycling, of course, and particularly jogging — people trying to get in shape, escaping from these tall office buildings and getting down here into the park. I suppose it's easily the most popular place in the city, and it's always here. An oasis. If it weren't for the park, I don't think New Yorkers could survive.

Central Park

As a sports journalist, I've always felt a very particular affinity with another athletic centre —Yankee Stadium. Even empty it seems full of sensations. I wouldn't dare step between the pitcher's mound and home plate—fifty summers of pitches have gone down there, and there must be some sort of current left by that. As a kid I used to go out onto the mound after a game and throw imaginary pitches. I'd have time to throw about three to Joe DiMaggio before the next kid jostled me off and took his turn.

Yankee Stadium

One of the peculiar manias of New Yorkers is their insistence on tearing down buildings, sometimes perfectly good buildings, and putting up others in their place. Grand Central Station, one of the greatest buildings in the world, is an example. The planners took one look at it, saw all that empty space inside, and decided they had to fill it with honeycombs full of workers. The wrecking balls were polished up and attached to the cranes, all set to go. But fortunately there is also in New York a great number of people who feel very strongly about the traditions and monuments of the past. So committees were formed and voices were raised and the great terminal was saved, even though they did balance a honeycomb on top of it. While the famous Flatiron Building in midtown Manhattan is obviously too imposing and beautiful to be menaced by developers or neglect, other landmarks and neighbourhoods are threatened. Harlem was once the great Rialto of Upper Manhattan, vibrant, active, friendly, with the people out in the streets in the evening. But now it's a place on the way down, a place with the machinery barely ticking over, a place to be rescued.

Opposite page   Grand Central Station
Right   The Flatiron Building

At the Columbia Avenue Street Fair, all the world's a stage, a carnival. Just about anybody can perform here, and it's easier because there aren't any tensions. You can fail miserably and nobody minds; it's the community spirit that matters, the sharing of an experience without pressure.

A New York fair's quite different from a country fair where there's bargaining and buying and selling going on. Here in New York, a fair is another safety valve the people have created for themselves, a microcosm of what they seem to need to help themselves get along with each other. Two hundred thousand people come along to the fair to enjoy the spirit of this city and its sense of togetherness.

I've lived in a number of capitals around the world, London and Paris, and in a number of culturally exotic cities, such as Venice and Bangkok, but I've always become just a little tired of them after a while. They become mere backgrounds and lose

their presence and their force. But not New York. You can't live in this city without feeling its impact day after day. Now there are New Yorkers who pretend not to, who try to be very blasé. But it has always seemed to me that people like that are in fact quite dazed by living in this community, a community where the ordinary is really rather hard to come by, and where the extraordinary is commonplace. So honestly, I'd feel the less for not having this spectacular city to come home to.

R.D. LAING'S
Glasgow

R.D. LAING'S
Glasgow

Glasgow is a place of stark, clashing contrasts. But such contradiction is the stuff of drama, creation, imagination. Glasgow has all that compacted intensely — in its commerce, its industry, its learning, and its people; in its violence and tenderness and great warmheartedness. I lived in this city for the first twenty-five years of my life. . . .

Glasgow Civic Centre

Glasgow was the second largest city of the greatest empire of the nineteenth century. The Glasgow Civic Centre, opened by Queen Victoria in 1888, is a fitting expression of Glasgow at its most prosperous.

Inside was this explosion of marble grandeur; outside, at least a hundred thousand people were living—and dying—in the most appalling slums.

When those city chambers were being built, one-quarter of the population of Glasgow lived in tenement blocks like these. This surviving block is a particularly pleasant example; the worst of them have already been torn down. A typical tenement block was four storeys high: you entered it by a "close", from which a stairway led upwards; on each of the four levels were four doors, each leading into a small single room, and in each of these single rooms a whole family would live, seven to fifteen people—and they would count themselves lucky to have a roof over their heads.

They came in the thousands from the Western Isles, from the Highlands, and from Ireland—driven by starvation and poverty—to provide the cheap labour upon which Glasgow based its prosperity. They were factory fodder. When these places were built to house them, there was no water, no taps, no bath, no toilet. Excrement was thrown out the window. People suffered from chronic malnutrition and vitamin deficiencies that produced, for instance, the Glasgow type, the stunted Glasgow "Wee Bacco" who had never grown because his bones hadn't been formed, bow-legged and with a hard head that was used to butt people in a fight.

Darkness, desolation, life pared down to the bone; mere existence, bare survival. And culture? Where in that world was there a place for Bach or Chopin?

The Gorbels

I wasn't born in a slum. I was born in a respectable neighbourhood not very far away. But if I had even dreamed of going "down there", I would have been thrashed by my father to within an inch of my life, because my parents were terrified that I would contract some of the contagious, unspeakable, unimaginable diseases "people down there" were riven and rotten with. This is where I was born, this was my "close", this is where I spent the first twenty-three years of my life. And here imagination and culture were just feasible, just possible. My mother played the piano, and later I played it too. My father sang; in fact, he was the first person to sing in Italian over the Scottish radio.

I don't think this is a godforsaken hole now, but I often thought it was then. How was I ever going to get out of it? Imagination, the mind, books? Well, there was a public library just across the road, and on top of it was an angel in the sky that I could gaze at from my bedroom window.

Glasgow is a city of parks, with over five dozen within its boundaries. For a city of its reputed violence, it is perhaps surprising that these are such safe places, places where the young and the old can come without fear, where lovers can be romantic. A hundred years ago they introduced bandstands into our parks, and every other night during the summer one could go and listen to a band or to entertainers. As a city boy who grew up surrounded by asphalt, I never needed to miss the country with all those parks around.

Glasgow does have that reputation for violence, but thank God the violence has stayed comparatively primitive. Fists, razor blades, knives, bicycle chains — mild compared to the more sophisticated things that are thrown around in some other cities. So far, no urban terrorism has developed here.

Walking around Glasgow one might not sense the wildness, the passion of the city. We haven't tribal dances or Mardi Gras or Saturnalia or even a Witches' Sabbath now; no more gladiators or Christians fed to the lions; but — for men, at least — we have the next best thing in these times of tranquillity and peace, the football matches.

A hundred years ago, Glasgow was called the Paris of the North, and sailing up the Clyde was a memorable experience. But now Glasgow has become a place more of industry than of beauty. At one time seventy per cent of the world's rolling stock came from this area and half the ships sailing the oceans of the world were built on Clydeside. My father and grandfather were Vikings; they didn't regard themselves as Scottish. Ships and machinery were in their blood. My father was an apprentice in a shipyard before the First World War and then went into the war to work with tanks and later with aircraft engines. By the time the war was over, he had come to detest not only war but what he felt machines did to the lives of the people who made them.

John Knox came to Glasgow after his stint as a galley slave, and his severe religious spirit still looms over the city, echoing with the thunder of the Reformation. Glasgow has not been a great patron of the arts; beauty, elegance, grace, proportion have seemed to many Glaswegians almost ungodly, competing with God or insulting Him by gilding the lily. Art is suspected of not being serious enough. But about what? That is what I have often wondered.

A Mackintosh grammar school

Glasgow was my first sample of the world. I looked at the faces of the buildings: what was the mind behind them? What was it all in aid of? What was it all about? What was Glasgow all about? To survive here, elegance had to be really tough. But this city had given birth to at least one extraordinary architect, though he was never given a real chance to impress his stamp on the city. His name was Charles Rennie Mackintosh.

The appearance of the Glasgow Art School, which was designed by Mackintosh, expresses the mind behind it. Inside is the library of the school, also designed by Mackintosh, and completed in 1909. Here I feel that the tensions of the Scottish character find perfect synthesis: its wildness and austerity, its softness and ruggedness, come together in perfect proportion.

It is a very congenial place to be in. Nothing in it cries out for attention, but everything is just right and it seems more right the more one looks at it. Correct without ever being cold. Those hanging lampshades are metal but they are not metallic. I wonder why the designers of our highrise brutalism haven't taken a leaf from Mackintosh's book. But maybe they haven't loved, as he did, the flowers and plants that he spent so much time studying and drawing and painting as a boy. Somehow he manages to take metal and use it organically and poetically to express through it light and colour and delight.

The Glasgow Art School library

Hugh MacDiarmid was one of Scotland's greatest poets and lived in a small cottage in the hills near Glasgow. On a plaque near the door is inscribed "The Little White Rose", one of his most famous poems:

The rose of all the world is not for me
I want for my part
Only the little white rose of Scotland
That smells sharp and sweet — and breaks the
    heart.

Perhaps genius has something to do with being able to live out in one's own person contradictions and conflicts that can tear whole peoples apart. MacDiarmid, an incorrigible freethinker, endorses what to most of us seems one of the most repressive regimes in the

world, Communism. Like almost all Scots, he is in fervent favour of Scottish nationalism. This sentiment is usually translated into political terms, but MacDiarmid has given his literary life to writing in a synthetic Scottish language, called Lallans, that he has virtually invented. Whether this is a lost cause or not, time alone will tell.

Sitting beside his fire, he recites a poem, "Lourd On My Hert", which is Lallans for "Heavy On My Heart" and which reflects his own uncertainty about Scotland's future:

Lourd on my hert as winter lies
The state that Scotland's in the day,
Spring to the North has aye come slow
But noo dour winter's like to stay
For guid,
And no' for guid!
O wae's me on the weary days
When it is scarce grey licht at noon;
It maun be a' the stupid folk

Diffusin' their dullness roon and roon
Like soot
That keeps the sunlicht oot.
Nae wonder if I think I see
A lichter shadow than the neist
I'm fain to cry: "The dawn, the dawn!
I see it brakin in the East."
But ah
— It's juist mair snaw!

The dead have one of the best views of Glasgow. As a medical student at The Royal Infirmary, I used to come to this cemetery to munch my lunchtime sandwiches in distinguished company. And to brood poetically over what it was all about:

To live *our life's the great adventure: fit*
For any hero. Nothing else can be
The meaning of our absurd mystery.
We'd like to think that there's some benefit
Somewhere, to something, someone, to the
    All,
That we're such sacks of comic lust: or good
For us that we are thus.

    At least we're food
For worms. However spirit fail, the call
Of death's a reconciliation for
Our flesh, its *contribution to the feast*
Which we partake of. Eater eaten, beast
For beast. From dust to dust. No less, no more.

We can be sure of death's utility,
Whatever we've accomplished of futility.

Even with the price of whisky these days, it is still said that the cheapest and quickest way out of Glasgow is two large whiskies; the sort of exit most Glaswegians would choose.

In a way there are as many Glasgows as there are eyes to see it. It is a diamond with as many facets as there are people in it. With all its many sides and divisions, Glasgow is still a place where you can enjoy a sense of community that is very rare in the great cities of the world nowadays. As a student and later, I shared a delightful experience of camaraderie and conviviality unlike anything I have come across any-where else. I once asked a man from Liverpool why he was living in London, and he said it was just because he wanted to be nearer to the centre of reality. But what was the centre of reality? The Changing of the Guard at Buckingham Palace? Well, no Glasgow man would ever dream of leaving Glasgow in order to find the centre of reality elsewhere. The centre of reality is where one's heart is.

GLENN GOULD'S
Toronto

GLENN GOULD'S
Toronto

I was born in Toronto, and it's been home base all my life. I'm not quite sure why; it's primarily a matter of convenience, I suppose. I'm not really cut out for city living and, given my druthers, I would avoid all cities and simply live in the country.

Yorkville

Toronto does belong on a very short list of cities I've visited that seem to offer to me, at any rate, peace of mind—cities which, for want of a better definition, do not impose their "cityness" upon you. Leningrad is probably the best example of the truly peaceful city. I think that, if I could come to grips with the language and the political system, I could live a very productive life in Leningrad. On the other hand, I'd have a crack-up for sure if I were compelled to live in Rome or New York—and of course, any Torontonian worthy of the name feels that way about Montreal, on principle.

The point is that, by design, I have very little contact with this city. In some respects, indeed, I think that the only Toronto I really know well is the one I carry about with me in

memory. And most of the images in my
memory-bank have to do with Toronto of the
forties and early fifties when I was a teenager.

Toronto's had a remarkably good press in
recent years. It has been called "the new, great
city", or "a model of the alternative future",
and not by Torontonians; these delightful
epithets have come from American and
European magazines and city planners. But
then Toronto has traditionally garnered very
favourable comments from visitors: Charles
Dickens dropped by in 1842 and remarked that
"the town is full of life, and motion, bustle,
business and improvement". Canadians, by
and large, are less complimentary; until very
recently, "Hogtown" was the preferred
description of Toronto by Canadians from
other parts of the country, and it has been said
that one of the few unifying factors, in this very
divided land, is that all Canadians share a
dislike — however perverse and irrational it may
be — for Toronto.

When the St. Lawrence Seaway was completed in 1959, Toronto — though seven hundred miles up-lake and up-river from the Atlantic Ocean — became, in effect, a deep-sea port. I've always been an incorrigible boat-watcher, and I can still remember, when the Seaway had been completed, how exciting it was to prowl the Toronto waterfront and encounter ships that had brought

Volkswagens from Germany or TV sets from Japan, and had names like *Wolfgang Russ* or *Munishima Maru*.

But well before the Seaway was completed, Toronto had already become international in another way. At the end of the Second World War, there was a great migration to Canada from all over the world — particularly from Europe and Asia — and a good percentage of those immigrants opted for Toronto. As a result of that the population of the city, which had been predominantly Anglo-Saxon, underwent a profound sea-change. The Anglo-Saxons were reduced to a minority, though still the largest minority to be sure, and the city began to reflect the cultural diversity of its new residents.

In 1793 Toronto's founder, Lieutenant-Governor John Graves Simcoe, predicted that the settlement would become a "palladium of British loyalty". And of his plans for the town, Simcoe wrote: "There was to be one church, one university to guard the Constitution, at every street corner a sentry, the very stones were to sing 'God Save The King'."

In Canadian political life, there's a saying, now almost a cliché, that Canada is a "political mosaic". The point of this expression is to enable us to distinguish ourselves from the Americans, who are fond of describing their society as a "melting pot", and the implication is that in Canada (and nowhere better exemplified than in Toronto), however intense the heat, we do not melt.

Toronto is situated on the north shore of Lake Ontario, the most easterly and also the smallest of the Great Lakes. But it's a sizeable pond, nonetheless. As a matter of fact, a Dutch friend of mine never tires of telling his relatives back home that you could drop all of Holland into this lake and still have room for enough windmills to keep Don Quixote busy for a lifetime. Actually he's wrong: I looked it up and Holland is almost twice as large as Lake Ontario. So you could drop it into Lake Superior, or Lake Michigan, or Lake Huron and it would disappear without a trace, but if you tried it here there would be very serious flooding.

A series of small islands overlap with one another like a crossword puzzle and protect Toronto Bay. The

islands are primarily a recreational area and, during the summer, ferryboats shuttle visitors and picnicking Torontonians back and forth across the harbour. But some hardy folks actually live on the islands all year round; in fact, there's been an island community of some sort for a century and a half.

Toronto's rationale as a city, indeed, is linked inevitably with its strategic location on Lake Ontario and, specifically, with its very fine harbour. After the American Revolution, the British were shopping around for likely spots to defend against the newly liberated colonists across the lake, and they elected to build a fort here. As an outpost of Empire, however, Fort York was by no means an unqualified success; the Americans sacked the town during the War of 1812.

Toronto's relationship with the American cities to the south, such as Buffalo which is forty miles across the lake, has often been the butt of local jokes. In my youth it was said that for a really lively weekend, what you had to do was drive to Buffalo. Nowadays Torontonians do not seem to feel that that migration serves any useful purpose, but we still seem to have some deep-seated psychological need to *look* at Buffalo every now and then. So, in 1976 we built a tower which, according to the tourist guides, is the tallest free-standing structure in the world. And they tell me that from up there, on a clear day, you can see — if not forever — at least to Buffalo.

C.N. Tower

There is no better example of the old Toronto versus the new than that shown by our two city halls, which stand on adjacent properties. The Old City Hall, which was finished in 1899, was built by a Canadian by the name of E.J. Lennox; he spent twelve years on the project and, by way of preliminary research, took a busman's holiday in Pennsylvania where he was apparently inspired by the then new jail in Pittsburgh. When I was in that city once on a concert tour (which is the musical equivalent of a penitentiary sentence), I happened to take a walk past that jail and, I must say, it looks not unlike our Old City Hall. Lennox maintained a remarkably consistent view of the appropriate enclosure for sinners and civil servants.

New City Hall was built in the early 1960s by the Finnish architect, Viljo Revell. He died, very prematurely, just after his building was completed, and it was said at the time that his death might well have been hastened by the howls of outrage with which some of Toronto's

elected officials greeted his remarkably imaginative design.

Toronto, at that time, was not exactly an hospitable place for contemporary art of any sort, and the decision to situate a large sculpture by Henry Moore in front of the New City Hall was the straw that broke the political camel's back. In fact, it was largely responsible for the electoral defeat of the mayor who supported its purchase. His chief opponent proclaimed that "Torontonians do not want abstract art shoved down their throats," and, of course, won the subsequent election handily.

Perhaps one indication of the remarkable change in Toronto's outlook during the last decade is that we now possess the largest collection of sculptures by Henry Moore in the western hemisphere; oddly enough, in view of all the earlier fuss, the collection was initiated by a gift from the sculptor himself. We Torontonians do have a way of ingratiating ourselves, I must say.

Top Henry Moore's *The Archer*
Bottom Part of the Moore collection

Opposite page
Top New City Hall
Bottom Old City Hall

Beneath Toronto's towering bank buildings can be found underground shopping malls that one can follow throughout the better part of downtown, and it is similarly possible to walk through the city, out of doors, by following a network of ravines and river valleys, without once setting foot on concrete. Down the largest of these ravines runs the River Don, locally known as "the Muddy Don". It empties into Toronto Harbour and, if I were in marathon training, it would be possible for me to walk seventeen miles to its source without making direct contact with the city—although it would, of course, be all around me.

Another route to follow is Yonge Street, Toronto's original north-south artery, which demarcates east side from west side in much the same way that Fifth Avenue divides Manhattan. It was the trail by which settlers went north in the early years of the nineteenth century to homestead, and a favourite boast of local press agents is that it is, in fact, the longest street in the world. They arrive at this particular bit of propaganda by virtue of the fact that Yonge Street doesn't exactly end; it just sort of dissolves into the Ontario highway system, and it is possible to follow this road, north and west, for about twelve hundred miles (almost two thousand kilometres). Most of those miles traverse country that is absolutely haunting in its emptiness and bleakness and starkly magnificent beauty.

But the garish beginning of Yonge Street is not one of those miles. It's a bit of the street known as "The Strip"; I'm not sure who coined the name or whether he was aware of the *double entendre* involved. On a smaller scale, these few blocks pose for Toronto the same problems that 42nd Street and Broadway create in New York. Civil libertarians find "The Strip" an irresistible cause; most of us simply find it an embarrassment.

"The Strip"

Ontario Place

Opposite page (bottom)　Lobby of the Royal
Bank Plaza

Perhaps the single most important influence on Toronto during the sixties was, in fact, something that took place over three hundred miles away, in Montreal. That city played host in 1967 to the World's Fair, which was called Expo '67. The two towns, Montreal and Toronto, have always had a sort of anything-you-can-build-I-can-build-better rivalry, and Toronto subsequently became determined to create its own Expo — if necessary, block by block. Perhaps our most Expo-like construction is a recreational area on the lakeshore, which is called Ontario Place.

Montreal's Expo was, of course, anything but an exercise in architectural consistency — it was actually a

very eclectic assembly of buildings—and Toronto's substitute Expo has employed similar contrasts.

Toronto, by general consensus, is the financial capital of Canada. The contending office towers that dominate the downtown district house major banking institutions, and most of them are located on or near Bay Street, which is the Canadian equivalent of America's Wall Street. People who are not particularly fond of Toronto insist that we go about the making of money with a religious devotion. I don't think that that's more true of this city than of most others, but if it is, then I suppose that other cliché—the one about such buildings being cathedrals of finance—would have to be given its due as well. In any case, most of us do our banking at very modest branch offices which, if the analogy must be pursued, are obviously parish churches.

A peculiar and important aspect of the Toronto mentality is a tendency to retain, even during times of radical change, a certain perspective, a certain detachment, a healthy scepticism about change for change's sake. I think it was probably that tendency which enabled Toronto to survive the sixties, when comparable cities south of the border were, quite literally, falling apart in both architectural and human terms. Toronto emerged from that turbulent decade as, arguably, one of the great cities of the world, certainly as an extraordinarily clean, safe, quiet, considerate sort of place in which to live.

It is called the Eaton Centre and
some people say it is Toronto's
answer to the Galleria in Milan; but
whether that's true or not, it certainly
is not your average Ma and Pa Kettle
corner store. It is in fact the flagship
of a vast retail empire which, despite
its monumentality, has remained a
family concern. The family con-
cerned are the Eatons and they have
been the leading lights of Toronto's,
and indeed Canada's, merchandizing
for the better part of a century.

Timothy Eaton, founder of the
business — who sits in bronze at the
entrance to the vast new store — was
always willing to gamble on somewhat off-the-beaten-track locations;
sometimes a move of only a few

blocks was involved, but Timothy always had the feeling that if he located his stores where shoppers were, by the time he had finished building them (usually an expansive as well as expensive operation) that's where the shoppers wouldn't be. Well, perhaps the descendants who run his empire now know something we don't: the new Eaton Centre is located, improbably enough, kitty-corner from the Yonge Street "Strip". Having cost almost a quarter of a billion dollars, it could be that it will revitalize this rather seedy quarter of Toronto. We can only hope so.

When I was a child, and indeed until very recently, this city was referred to as "Toronto the Good". The reference was to the city's puritan traditions: one could not, for example, attend concerts on Sunday until the 1960s; it was not permissible to serve alcohol in any public place on the Sabbath until very recently; and now a furor has developed at City Hall over the issue of whether Torontonians should be permitted to drink beer at baseball games.

But you have to understand that, as an anti-athletic, non-concertgoing teetotaller, I approve all such restrictions. I, perhaps, rather than the hero of George Santayana's famous novel, am "The Last Puritan". So I always felt that "Toronto the Good" was a very nice nickname. On the other hand, a lot of my fellow citizens became very upset about it and tried to prove that we could be just as bad as any other place.

Above and opposite page (top)   The Eaton Centre

Opposite page (bottom)   Timothy Eaton

Toronto incorporates five boroughs which form a sort of satellite network around the original city. North York, which recently incorporated itself as a city, is the largest of these and houses about half a million people. It is my favourite area of the city by far, and although I live downtown, I keep a studio in North York. I think what attracts me to it is the fact that it offers a certain anonymity; it has a sort of improbable, Brasilia-like quality. In fact, it has much of the tensionless atmosphere of one of those capital cities where the only business is the business of government and which are deliberately located away from the geographical mainstream — Ottawa, say, or Canberra.

During the fifties and sixties, North York seemed to spring spontaneously from the soil; I can remember when the area was all farmland. And what developed was a community so carefully planned, so controlled in its density, in the structural and rhythmical regularity with which its homes, offices, shops, and public buildings come together, that it doesn't seem like a city at all; which, needless to say, is the highest compliment I can pay it. To me it seems, as I have said, like a seat of government; or perhaps, rather better, like a vast company town, presided over by an autocratic but benevolent Chairman of the Board, whose only order of the day, every day, is — Tranquillity.

It is fashionable to downgrade suburbia these days, of course. The march back to city centre, with all its zooty renovated row houses, is all the rage, I know; but this part of Toronto, I think, represents the North American suburban dream at its best. And I love it!

In my youth, Toronto was also called "The City of Churches" and, indeed, the most vivid of my childhood memories in connection with Toronto have to do with churches. They have to do with Sunday evening services, with evening light filtered through stained-glass windows, and with ministers who concluded their benediction with the phrase: "Lord, give us the peace that the earth cannot give." Monday mornings, you see, meant that one had to go back to school and encounter all sorts of terrifying situations out *there* in the city. So those moments of Sunday evening sanctuary became very special to me; they meant that one could find a certain tranquillity—even in the city—but only if one opted not to be part of it.

Well, I don't go to church these days, I must confess, but I do repeat that phrase to myself very often—the one about the peace that the earth cannot give—and find it a great comfort. What I've done, I think, while living here, is to concoct some sort of metaphoric stained-glass window, which allows me to survive what appear to me to be the perils of the city—much as I survived Monday mornings in the schoolroom. And the best thing I can say about Toronto is that it doesn't seem to intrude upon this hermit-like process.

It's been fascinating to get to know Toronto, after all these years, but not even this exploration of it has made me a city convert, I'm afraid. I am more than ever convinced, though, that like Leningrad, Toronto is essentially a truly peaceful city.

But perhaps I see it through rose-coloured glasses; perhaps what I see is still so controlled by my memory that it's nothing more than a mirage. I hope not though, because if that mirage were ever to evaporate, I should have no alternative but to leave town.

JONATHAN MILLER'S
London

JONATHAN MILLER'S
London

I know this is the kind of picture you expect to see at the start of an illustrated essay about London. In a way the glamour of royal pageantry is a form of tourist show business; show business of a very high order admittedly, and you have got to be a hard man indeed to resist the spectacle. But my only reason for including these guardsmen is that my grandfather, a Russian Jew who came to London in the 1860s, was a Fournier Street furrier who supplied the fur for the busbys the soldiers are wearing.

Like the great church built by Nicholas Hawksmoor nearby, Fournier Street — in the middle of Whitechapel in London's East End — has known rather better days. And the odd thing about the street, despite its august English eighteenth-century appearance, is that it has never known a truly English population. It first housed French Huguenot weavers, who came here after fleeing religious persecution in France; then, in the middle of the nineteenth century, Jews from Eastern Europe came to set up in trade. And now, in the middle of the twentieth century, Indians and Pakistanis have come. It was to one of the houses on this street that my father's father came from Russia in the 1860s and established a fur-trading business, importing among other furs the bearskins for guardsmen's busbys.

I have never been able to find out exactly which of the houses on Fournier Street my grandfather owned, but he must have lived here for fifteen or twenty years. By the time he had been here ten years he was sufficiently prosperous to have ambitions to be an English country gentleman. My father tells me that when he was a child about 1900, they already had a pony and trap. The problem was that they had no easy access to the stables at the back of the house; so the horse had to be taken in through the front door, blindfolded by a shawl wrapped round its head to stop it shying at the cut-glass chandeliers in the drawingroom as it passed by.

Fournier Street

Opposite page   Christ Church Spitalfields

Interior of the synagogue in Gracechurch
Street

It must be thirty years since I was last
in the synagogue in Gracechurch
Street. I always went to synagogue
rather unwillingly anyway, and when
my father insisted I make an appearance — at least on the high holidays —
it was always to that building I went
rather than to our local synagogue,
not drawn by any particular feature of
it or by the prayers, but probably by
its architectural gracefulness. Perhaps
its very Englishness attracted me. It
was built by a Quaker architect in
1701, the first synagogue constructed
for a Jewish community in England.

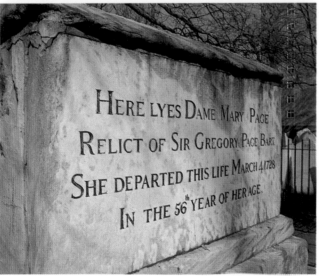

It was built for a congregation of Dutch and Portuguese Jews who had come from Holland and had first met for the Sabbath in a small house nearby in Gracechurch Street. The candelabra were brought from Amsterdam by the Dutch members of the congregation. One can imagine what it must have looked like in the early years of the nineteenth century when the benches were filled with Dutch and Portuguese Jews, but by the time I came here the local community had dwindled to fifty or sixty. The rest had spread out and been assimilated into London, gradually taking their part in English life, as indeed I have done.

One of the things that is nice about England, or that has been until recently, is its ability to absorb and transform all those who come from abroad, and to turn them into Englishmen after a while. Perhaps for most Londoners an old graveyard such as Bunhill Fields is nothing more than a wistful reminder of the shortness of human life. But for someone like myself, who has only gradually come to feel like an Englishman, the tombstones with their names going back for centuries are an unsettling reminder of the shortness of my past as an Englishman. How nice it would be if I could look around and find ancestors of mine who were born in the eighteenth century—an English past —something I'll never have.

Bunhill Fields

John Nash's Park Crescent

To make this story of assimilation a bit more dramatic, I should like to be able to say that my father made one single leap from the immigrant East End to the fashionable West End of London. But, of course, it is not quite as simple as that. My father's family had already begun to move towards the prosperous north of the city by the start of the twentieth century. And by 1930 my father had established himself as a fairly successful psychiatrist and set up home and consulting room in the rather privileged enclave of Park Crescent, to which I, having been born on Harley Street nearby, was brought as a squalling infant.

Park Crescent is part of one of the most interesting and ambitious town-planning schemes ever to be inflicted on London. It was built by the architect John Nash, who until 1798 had been a fairly unsuccessful speculative designer and builder. About that time, he made a rather strategic marriage with a prosperous woman who introduced him to the Prince Regent, who happened to have ambitions to impose on London a design similar to that of Napoleonic Paris. And Nash promised him something of that sort.

What Nash devised was a series of grand circuses and approaches from Carlton House Terrace in the south, where the Prince Regent lived, all the way up Regent Street, to the Park here in the north. Park Crescent is all that remains of a grand circus, but there are beautiful terraces which go right the way round Regent's Park, and beautiful villages beyond them on either side.

One of the things that always startles and surprises me is how unvisited this place is. When you look at it, it is just as grand as Leningrad, which was built at more or less the same time, and it is just as imposing as the Champs Elysées. It is a huge flamboyant spectacle, not architecture but theatrical scenery. Nash's sense of the theatrical and picturesque never deserted him.

Carlton House Terrace

Soane Museum

Opposite page (top and bottom right) Breakfast room
(bottom left) Architectural collection

I have always thought that the most interesting and attractive sights in London are the ones which are so public and obvious that everyone passes them without noticing them — such as those extraordinarily spacious parks and terraces which really are London — and on the other hand, the quaint private places such as the Soane Museum.

Sir John Soane was one of the finest architects of the late eighteenth century, responsible for building part of the Bank of England and the stables at Chelsea Barracks. But perhaps his most interesting monument is the place he designed for himself in Lincoln's Inn Fields, which is both a private residence and a museum. Each room has its own characteristic feature. For instance his breakfast room is studded with mirrors from each of which you can have a complete view of the whole room. I first saw this room twenty years ago, and I was so excited by it that when I made a film of *Alice in Wonderland* a few years later, I set one of the scenes in this room.

Eventually Soane took over two neighbouring houses to accommodate his collections. In another room that is a favourite of mine is hung William Hogarth's famous series of paintings, *The Rake's Progress*, on which Stravinsky based his equally famous opera. And because there is no more room on the walls, Soane's own architectural drawings for the Bank of England and other projects are hung on hinged panels.

I've always felt that the most exotic form of tourism is to be given the chance of revisiting the city in which one actually lives, really seeing it for the first time. You see, the problem of a big city is that the visitor is always seeing the official sites, the spectacles, observing it from points of view from which it was meant to be seen. And those of us who live here gradually grow indifferent to what it looks like, and it becomes more or less invisible. So what one needs is to look at the city in a way it was never meant to be looked at. And the best way of doing that is to travel along the North London railway line from Broad Street to Kew.

I've known this route ever since I was a child. But in those days I was too busy larking around and showing off to girls to notice what could be seen along the line. In recent years, though, I've had an opportunity of seeing it from a rather unusual point of view; ever since I left medicine and got involved in show business, I've been travelling on this line against the rush hour, going out to slightly disreputable rehearsal rooms on the edge of London. So I've had the chance of sitting in empty carriages, looking at the city at moments when it is more or less caught unawares, when it has let its hair down and is in a slightly informal mood — at a time when it is not meant to be looked at.

If this mysterious railway journey is an exercise in studying the invisible, it brings you eventually to something which is pure spectacle, pure exhibi-

Top   North London railway line

tion, one of the grandest, certainly one of the most refined spectacles in London. It is the great Palm House in Kew Gardens, which was erected in the middle of the nineteenth century to house tropical plants and palms. Originally it was called the Palm Stove, and with its great poised transparency, it is a paragon of visibility. What I like about it is the way it expresses that English love of contradiction and paradox — high Lewis Carroll fantasy and hard, down-to-earth engineering; the materials from which it is made, the strongest and the most brittle — iron and glass. And also I like the way in which its form seems to take some inspiration from the very palms it houses.

Opposite page and below The Palm House in Kew Gardens

The Royal Naval Hospital

If you are not addicted to such industrial splendours as the huge oil refineries down the estuary, then I suppose the most pleasing vista on the lower reach of the Thames is the Royal Naval Hospital at Greenwich. It was originally established at the end of the seventeenth century by Charles II as a hospital for seamen. Later on it was taken over as a college where naval officers could learn to take their place on the cruel sea. But it is also a jolly good spot to see two other rather nice architectural splendours. In the gap between the two halves of the college, a building by Inigo Jones can be seen which is known as Queen Anne's House. And behind, on the very top of the hill, is perhaps the most famous building of all, the Royal Observatory, from which Greenwich Mean Time is measured.

Sir Christopher Wren, who might as well have been an astronomer as an architect, is said to have played a large part in designing this graceful observatory for the Royal Society, of which he was one of the founding members. The Society was granted its charter by Charles II in the early 1660s, after he was restored to the throne. Its aim was to investigate science and to provide solutions for certain practical problems. One of the most pressing of these was the measuring of longitude at sea, which demanded accurate astronomical observations. And associated with this was the need to establish fixed time and a meridian from which to take observations.

There is nothing particularly magical about the meridian at Greenwich, which is a brass strip inset in the ground that runs across the site of the observatory. While it was important to have some fixed point from which to measure lapsed time, it could have been a few yards away or five miles off, or even in another country. It was a measure of England's place in the world that the meridian was finally established here at Greenwich. And it is a sad commentary on the state of England today that our influence has been reduced to this single line from which the world agreed to measure the passage of time.

Royal Observatory

Almost two hundred years ago, the poet Wordsworth claimed that "earth had not anything to show more fair" than the view you could get of the Houses of Parliament from Westminster Bridge. I am not certain that he would hold the same opinion about the view along the river Thames today.

Air raids and then architecture have mutilated the gracefully sleeping scene and it is hard to understand what Wordsworth was talking about. After the Blitz, there was a great opportunity to develop the city and make the waterfront graceful again. But mindless modernism, married to commercial greed, missed the opportunity. The city is simply a ruined remnant of its former self.

In 1666 the old City of London was devastated by a great fire, and a tall monument still stands on the spot near the waterfront where the fire began. But as much as anything else, it commemorates the achievement of Sir Christopher Wren in rebuilding London after that fire.

During the Blitz, the dome of Wren's St. Paul's Cathedral was one of the inspiring emblems of the survival of Great Britain. It seems odd that after the war we should have failed to seize the opportunity of that destruction, to rebuild the city in the image which Sir Christopher had made during the seventeenth century.

There is one landmark that has been saved — Tower Bridge. For all its absurd and monstrous inconvenience, it is so famous that they have been shamed into keeping it. They have even washed it, since it used to be as black with soot as the ace of spades. It is the last bridge across the Thames before you reach the unfenced emptiness of the English Channel. The official sights and monuments of London fall behind and the river broadens out to an industrial shambles of ruined wharves and warehouses.

Top   Tower Bridge
Bottom   St. Paul's Cathedral

Opposite page
Top   Houses of Parliament
Bottom   Monument to the Great Fire

It seems appropriate to finish my
journey of rediscovery on the
enchanted slopes of Primrose Hill. All
sorts of people have come toiling up
its slopes, hoping for apocalyptic
visions of one kind or another.
William Blake came here and had
conversations with the spirit of the
sun; he thought that one of the pillars
of the New Jerusalem would be
planted on the summit of Primrose
Hill. Engels came here and looked
down over the southern vistas of
London, perhaps brooding over the
downfall of capitalism. And at the end
of *War of the Worlds*, H.G. Wells left
one of the Martian fighting machines
abandoned on the summit of the hill,
with pieces of extraterrestrial flesh
hanging from it.

But it is enchanted for all sorts of
reasons. It is a place where you have a
view, not only of space but also of
time. From here I get a strange,
foreshortened view of my family's
moves through London. Over to the
southeast, on the far edge of the city,
I can more or less see where my
grandfather came first and my father
was born. And in the middle distance
below, on the other side of the park,
where my father settled and I was
born. And on this side of the park, in
North London, where my children
were born and where they still play,
on Primrose Hill.

There have been changes in the
city below. When I first played here,
shortly after the war, the most
prominent feature on the skyline was
St. Paul's Cathedral, hanging out
there in the smoke. Now it is hard to

Primrose Hill

pick it out from among those high blocks of flats. The whole city is changing and it will go on changing. I have no idea what my children will see in twenty-five or thirty years' time. Perhaps, in any case, like me and my family, they will move further north, or elsewhere in England. Perhaps they may even leave England altogether.

HILDEGARD KNEF'S
Berlin

HILDEGARD KNEF'S
Berlin

Berlin has more bridges than Venice. So I was told by my grandfather. But I never saw those bridges then, for we lived near the railroad station in Wilmersdorf, one of the many boroughs of the city. I am one of the more than three million inhabitants of Berlin and, like many of us, I was not born here but only raised here.

Ruins of Annhalter Station

My grandfather was Polish, my father was
Flemish, and though my mother was born in
Berlin I hold a British passport. That makes a
Berliner.

One borough of the city, called Kreuzberg,
has turned Turkish because of the influx of
foreign "guest workers". Their children learn
German at Berlin schools and are totally
assimilated, but without the parents' ever
really becoming part of the city. They live their
own lives just as they would have done in
Ankara.

There is also a definite Slavic influence in
the Berlin character, and a French one going
back to the Huguenots, the Protestants of
France who took refuge here. To this day you

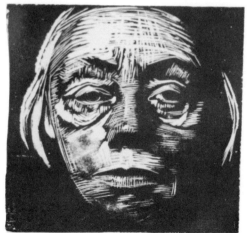

can still find many French names in the telephone book.

The famous 1920s spawned an explosion of artistic expression in Berlin, digging deep into the soul of man. Käthe Kollwitz in particular made her compassion heroic. She looked at Berlin's poor in a different way, transforming her suffering sensitivity into a proletarian heroism. Her work tells us about the craving for love in a world of turmoil.

I never knew the famous Romanisches Café, beside the Memorial Church, during the 1920s. That was the time when Max Reinhardt, Bertolt Brecht, and numerous other writers, actors, directors, and painters made Berlin the centre of cultural Europe—until Hitler took over and made the golden years into an inferno and sent the *crème de la crème* into exile. I learned of this era only after I arrived in the United States in 1947. I had not taken part in it. But I knew bombs, hunger, and imprisonment.

As I said, I lived in Wilmersdorf at the railroad station. My grandfather lived in the Frobenstrasse, one of the few streets in Berlin without trees. In this district lived Christopher Isherwood, catching the spirit of the times in his *Berlin Stories*. His most famous character is Sally Bowles of *Cabaret* fame. The first theatre to open in Berlin after the war was the Tribüne, under Victor de Kowa, where we performed a kind of cabaret.

I do remember the times when the Nazis shouted and the anti-Nazis kept silent because we, the young ones, might give them away. Of all things, I decided to become a painter just then. And I succeeded in getting a scholarship to the Art Academy, which was located in what today is East Berlin.

Olympic Stadium

Opposite page   Holocaust memorial

My father died when I was six months old. He was twenty-eight years old. Seven years later my mother got married again, to a man from Hanover who was a violent anti-Nazi. He was the owner of a factory in partnership with a man named Mr. Gold. Just about the time she married him, the Nazis came to power. When the Nazis advised my stepfather to join the party and get rid of Mr. Gold, he declined. A day later he had no factory.

Years later, when I came back from a Russian prison camp, my stepfather asked me, "Do you remember the day your class at school was taken to the Olympic Stadium? You had been

very impressed. Your mother said, 'Have you taken leave of your senses?' " I was only capable of remaining silent. The 1936 Olympics had been held here in Berlin and the world had watched as Hitler flexed his muscles. The children in my class who were Jewish suddenly disappeared. The teacher told us that they had moved to Poland.

During the war, most of the houses of my neighbourhood either vanished or were destroyed beyond recognition. When I saw the first house burning, I cried. From then on until the end of the war, except in theatre roles where it was asked for, I was unable to shed a tear.

The women of Berlin evoke the image of quick-lipped, long-legged fräuleins. But for me they mean also, indeed mainly, the *Trümmerfrauen* — those who kept Berlin going while the men were gone and who, after the war, cleaned the city of rubble, piece by piece and hand by hand.

Though Stalingrad had fallen and the war had become unbearable, I was oblivious of it all; I wanted to be an actress. Through the help of Else Bongers, my mentor since that time, I succeeded. My acting career started rather peculiarly. "Let me see your profile," said Else Bongers; then, "Can you give an audition?" "No," I whispered. "Why do you want to be an actress?" "Because I am talented," I said. "How do you know?" "I just know!"

In the winter of 1945-46 I performed at the Schlosspark Theatre, which had previously been a hicktown movie-house, but was converted into a fine theatre by a man called Barlog. People paid with nails so that we could build sets for our produc-

tions and then sat there shivering with us to forget the horror of their existence.

Nowadays the Kurfürstendamm is Berlin's main artery, a street of hotels, crazy sex shops, discotheques, and boutiques. But I cannot free myself of the memory of the German and Russian tanks rattling down the Kurfürstendamm for days on end and people running before the tanks, and bumping into the feet of soldiers hanged from lampposts with plaques around their necks marked: "I was too weak to die for my fatherland."

The Albrecht-Achilles-Strasse off the Kurfürstendamm is where I was sentenced to death for leaving my platoon. I was dressed as a boy soldier, hoping to escape many unpleasant things that were happening at that time in Berlin.

But even though I was freed when they discovered my true identity, I later ended up in a Russian prison camp. By going to the camp, I was one of the few to survive the Spandau massacre. The Russians had taken over the houses and the rest of the German army was trying to get out of Berlin, across the bridge. Most of them failed, and died.

Opposite page (bottom) and above Kurfürstendamm

But let me talk about the unscathed Berlin.

Actually it is an old town, founded in the Middle Ages. In 1688, there were nineteen thousand Berliners; Paris had a population of half a million. In the beginning of the eighteenth century, Berlin became the residence of princes, kings, and emperors, the official seat of the monarchy and the capital of Prussia. At the outbreak of the Second World War, the city had ballooned to over two million inhabitants.

The Brandenburg gate was built in the eighteenth century and shortly afterwards was crowned by a quadriga, a four-horse chariot, which was dragged away to Paris by Napoleon, only to be dragged back again to Berlin by Marshall Blücher after Napoleon's downfall. The travelling quadriga is now back where it started on top of the gate which is part of East Berlin.

The Reichstag building actually meant very little to me when I was young, except that I heard that it had played a part in Hitler's rise to power and that it was burned down by him with somebody else being held responsible.

Brandenburg Gate

The Reichstag

The Wall

Everything in Berlin is actually double. An East Zoo and a West Zoo, an East Opera and a West Opera, and just as many theatres in the East as in the West.

The wall dividing the city went up in 1961. Little can be said about something as monstrous as that. The soul of the city is divided, and even though we do not think of it continuously, there is still this sense of division in the back of our minds. Because of that, Berlin's energy has mellowed. But since it was overbearing before, it is still very prominent.

Berlin is famous for its humour, even if it has become a little less exuberant during the last few years. In spite of the wall, the city's nightlife is hectic. All the same, the Berlin reputation for decadence is a little bit overdone. It is more or less the same as in any other big city. No matter what your craving, you can live as well here as anywhere else. There are the same night-birds in the city, but nowhere else, except perhaps New York, do they find their prey so easily. Berlin has more live jazz clubs than any city in the world. For me, that makes it even more like New York.

The Rathaus Schöneberg, the city hall of Berlin, is where President John F. Kennedy made his famous "*Ich bin ein Berliner*" speech — "I am a Berliner." Shortly afterwards I was commissioned by the city's mayor at the time, Willy Brandt, to go to the United States to talk about the war and Berlin.

My whole family is buried in Berlin — my grandfather, my grandmother, my father, my stepfather, my mother, and my brothers. And I live here, because Berlin is a part of me and I am a part of Berlin.

Rathaus Schöneberg

GERMAINE GREER'S
Sydney

GERMAINE GREER'S
Sydney

Once a week, at least once a week, I dream about Sydney. I know it is a Sydney dream, first of all, because of the smells — the smell of the sea, the smell of the frangipani — because of the sounds — the sounds of the birds crying — and because of the feeling that the sky is so far away. In Europe, the sky sits on your head like a grey felt hat; in Australia, the sky is a million miles away and all that lies beneath it belongs to you.

Opposite page   Ben Buckler

There are many beautiful cities in the world, but I think that Sydney is the only one whose beauty still belongs to the people.

The heart of Sydney is the harbour, of course. And unlike other grand and beautiful ports, the harbour is still accessible to the people who want to use it: if they want to, they can sail on it, they can swim in it, they can drive surfmobiles on it, they can fish on it, or they can just pick up shellfish along its shores.

The harbour is the lungs of Sydney, keeping the city fresh and cool, and making its air like no other in the world.

It is not easy for me to tell about these things. I can only give an impression of a land of limitless possibilities, where whatever you want to do you can do, simply by force of wanting to do it. This is the city where the poorest people can be millionaires, where for practically nothing they can do the things that in other countries are limited to those who join select clubs and pay enormous membership fees and qualify in all kinds of obscure ways of blood and breeding. But in Sydney, if you want it, it is all yours.

It is an open city, welcoming to anybody who has some way of using its huge generosity, its amazing endowment of natural beauty. Its shores smell sweeter because the wind blows across thousands of miles of ocean to us: the trade winds, that for us do not just mean trade, but also mean the breath of life. They carry away much of our pollution, and

when Sydneysiders talk about pollution, those of us who have experi-
enced it elsewhere know that they
have been blessedly spared the
knowledge of what it actually is.

It may seem incredible, but when I first came to Sydney what I fell in love with was not the harbour or the gardens or anything else but a pub called The Royal George. Or, more particularly, with a group of people who used to go there every night and every weekend and sit there and talk and talk. They were completely different from the intelligentsia I got to know in Melbourne who always talked about art and truth and beauty and argument *ad hominem*; instead, these people talked about truth and only truth, insisting that most of what we were exposed to during the day was ideology, which was a synonym for lies — or bullshit, as they called it. I think what attracted me was their anarchist principles, which I had been practising on my own in Melbourne without any sort of support. In Sydney it was actually a way of life, an intolerably difficult discipline which I forced myself to learn, partly by spending the sunniest, most beautiful days closeted in that pub, in a room filthy with cigarette smoke and always smelling of stale beer, where we talked ourselves hoarse.

Another part of Sydney I loved from the start was the Harbour Bridge. I knew it from ashtrays and souvenirs, of course, but I was not prepared for its absolute beauty. It is not the biggest bridge in the world, or the highest, or the newest, or the oldest, but I think it is one of the most beautiful. I was especially attached to it because it was a sort of refuge. When I sometimes got miserable, with the people I lived with or with The Royal George, I used to run away to where the footpath was torn up on the bridge and climb down into the rigging underneath and sit waving my legs above the sea, where the wind called the southerly buster blew away all the crossness and all the arguments.

Harbour Bridge

World Series Cricket was the brain-
child of an Australian sportsman
called Kerry Packer. The whole idea
is that the game is meant to be
entertainment. I am not sure that I
actually like it very much. It is
strange to be under this darkening
sky, and it is very strange to feel cold
watching cricket in Australia. I think
the main thing is that it has shaken
cricket up all over the world. Aus-
tralians, and Sydneysiders in particular, have helped the world to understand that sportsmen these days are

not gentlemen using their time off for elegant diversion. They are more likely to be members of the working class who have achieved distinction in the only way that was open to them. They are working-class heroes, and at least Kerry Packer recognized that fact and gave cricket to the people in a form they could really enjoy. You used to have to be retired or unemployed to go to cricket in the daytime. Nowadays people who work for a living can come in the evening and see a match from start to finish.

Sydney has three race tracks, and I served a very hard apprenticeship on all three. For one whole year I had to come to every metropolitan race meeting; I had to bet on one horse, and one horse only, in every race; and I had to lay a uniform stake of five shillings, which went up to ten shillings after a while. The idea was that I was being taught how to make a living by gambling. By the end of the year I had discovered that I had broken even, which is quite the worst year's work I have ever done. I remember it was so boring that I could not bring myself to study the form. If I had stuck with it, instead of falling asleep over the form guide every Friday night, I could have been extremely rich now. I would probably be rather eccentric as well, because the people who taught me are now running a syndicate here from the paddock that keeps most of them very well-heeled and on which they pay no taxes at all, simply because they do not exist as earners in the country. It is extraordinary that this kind of banditry is still possible.

My dreary years of apprenticeship as a punter taught me something that has proved useful in later life: that there are two sorts of people in the world, the sort of people who like to win and the sort of people who like to lose. And, in fact, the second category outnumbers the first category. They actually used to come here for the melancholy pleasure of returning home broke, food money and everything gone. I think it is one of the most extraordinary things about

Australia, that you can go on losing
most of your life. There is a
phenomenon called loserism, which
means people always cut their
chances. It is something the women's
movement does, something that the
left wing does in America and in
England. They are terrified of actually betting on the right horse.

As I have said, everybody in Sydney is a millionaire, because whether a man has money or not he can do what millionaires pay millions to do. He can sail his boat, he can fish, he can play any sport he wants to play, and he can have children who in other parts of the world could only be the children of the very rich, children who are tall and strong and absolutely unafraid.

Sydneysiders talk about water the way the Swiss talk about snow. They go on and on about which wind was blowing, what kind of bottom there was, whether there were seaweeds or jellyfish. Their commonest concern is

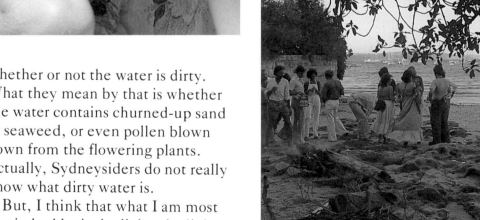

Bondi Beach

whether or not the water is dirty. What they mean by that is whether the water contains churned-up sand or seaweed, or even pollen blown down from the flowering plants. Actually, Sydneysiders do not really know what dirty water is.

But, I think that what I am most bewitched by is the light: the light that pours over everything, saturating everything, making even the most commonplace things seem beautiful. When you are living on the dark side of the world, this light is something that haunts you, day in and day out.

Sydney life is not all fun and games. Like
people everywhere, Sydneysiders have got to
earn a living. In some ways it is harder here
than elsewhere. Coming to work on the ferry
across the harbour must make the office seem
even more like a tomb. It is very revealing to
watch people on that ferry from Manly —
people coming to work: the shorts that a lot of
men wear, and the knees of Sydney — brown
knees with golden hair on them, which I love
to watch — and then a gentleman in a
pin-striped suit, reading the paper as if he were
on an English train somewhere in Kent,
commuting to London; and with the sea
sparkling all around, and people throwing
fishing-lines in the water; and then the people
getting off the ferry, some people carrying
surfboards and some carrying briefcases — it is
all just incredible.

There are some things that disturb me about
Sydney now. The new office-tower blocks
disturb me, especially the tower like a
hypodermic needle pointing to God. The
dullest cities in the world have those things
because they are terrified of not having any
appeal. They have to create an instant
monument. We do not need that; the harbour
is our monument. And I do not think we need
that kind of office accommodation. It destroys
the natural skyline and makes everything seem
small and squalid.

Nevertheless, something about Sydney over-
rides attempts by the City Fathers to turn it
into a wasteland and a collection of
mausoleums. Some sort of vitality. When it was
first suggested that Martin Place should be
turned into a pedestrian precinct, there was
terrific opposition from the commercial frater-
nity. However, as soon as the first bit of it was
finished, even before the newly planted trees
had grown, people began to gather there
spontaneously and it turned into what Sydney

Ferry from Manly

had never had—a town centre in the middle of
downtown, financial Sydney. Then they went
on with the plan until now we have four or five
blocks given over to pedestrians. It is not dead
after dark as in other cities; people still like to
come there and sit. And at lunchtime, there are
concerts.

Below   Martin Place

The first semidetached cottage in Sydney was built about 1850, and in fact not very many semidetached homes of any sort were ever built in the city. Like most of the early houses, it was built of stone and the extraordinary thing about it is that it has escaped being tarted up. Nowadays, tarting up has become the rule. Its marvellous overgrown garden goes down in steps to the harbour, and its huge *magnolia grandiflora* are as old as the house itself; they lend an extraordinary charm to a building that is entirely without pretension. The same cannot be said, alas, of some of the other houses in Balmain where the cottage stands, or indeed of the houses in Paddington, Woolloomooloo, and all the older inner areas of Sydney where the first settlements grew.

Sydney architects discovered the beauty of older houses in the 1960s. The houses built in the 1870s and 1880s are rather inconvenient, having only two rooms on the ground floor and two rooms on the upper floor, connected by a staircase. At first the kitchens were built outside because they burned down so often, but gradually they became attached to the main building; nowadays, with renovations, you find very elegant and proper arrangements for ablutions and cooking and that sort of thing. When I came here to live, I lived in one of the earliest homes to be done up, house-sitting for a renovator. There were no trees on the street, and the trees there now are only ten years old and were planted with such haste that nobody realized that their roots would later tear up the pavement. But the result is charming and what was once a rough area is now a centre of the bijou residence and the young executive aesthetic.

The dreary uniformity of the Glebe Housing Estate contrasts very oddly with the opaline variation seen in the privately owned houses. I should explain that all the little outhouses are

The Glebe Housing Estate

lavatories or, in Australian, dunnies. The
Housing Commission has installed indoor
bathrooms now, but in rather inconvenient
locations — downstairs behind the kitchen and
the laundry although everyone sleeps upstairs.

It is interesting to speculate what difference
it makes to the morale of people living in
rented public housing when they are not
allowed to express themselves through the
medium of their houses; all are painted exactly
alike.

Opposite page   Paddington

Sydney Opera House

In Australia now conservation is a magic word. And it is not just the authorities that are interested; even the trade unions take a militant stand on it. The reason why Sydney's startling new Opera House does not have a parking lot, it seems, is that the head of the Builders' Labour Union refused to have his men remove the plants and flowers from the botanical gardens on the shore nearby to dig out and construct the carpark, on which the gardens were to be replaced. And that is one of the encouraging things about this country. Things don't run in their accustomed channels. Workers do take action that is more usually associated with the ruling class, which may be because they are in fact the ruling class.

"There was never anything worthwhile made yet but by its own rules." Those words were written by a great Australian, a complete anarchist and a Sydneysider named Harry Hooton. I met him when I first came to Sydney and was walking about town in a black dress with red stockings on. He walked behind me for a long way and he told me afterwards he was proud of my red stockings, because they were in defiance of the current mode and customs of the city; in fact people used to hang out of cars and scream at me, "Who do you think you are?"

So I got to know Harry a bit, and he puzzled me a lot and said things that rather shocked me then. Alas, I understand him much better now. When I last saw him, he was dying, just a whisper of himself, but still enormous; the power of his soul filled the little room he lay in. And he called me to tell me that he had great faith in me, that he thought I was the woman of the twenty-first century. I didn't know what he meant then, but I think a lot of the things I've done since I've done out of a desire to please Harry Hooton. Too late. . . .

It was once said by one of Sydney's nasty columnists that I lost my virginity in Melbourne and my heart in Sydney. That's not exactly accurate. I lost my heart to a Sydneysider in Melbourne, and I followed him to Sydney to be with him. It was only afterwards that I fell in love with the city itself. And of all my love affairs, this is the one that looks like it is going to last me the rest of my life.

STUDS TERKEL'S
Chicago

STUDS TERKEL'S
Chicago

About twenty years ago I found myself lost in the town of Brescia, the home of Pope John XXIII, in northern Italy. I wandered into a restaurant, a *trattoria*, and there an old woman said to me, "Americano?" "Si, signora." "What city?" "Chicago, signora." "Chicago," she said, "boom boom, boom boom!" "No, signora," I said, "Chicago is more than that, far far more. . . ."

Louis Sullivan was *the* Chicago architect, and teacher of another famous architect, Frank Lloyd Wright, who called him *Leiber Meister*. He practised here in the 1890s and 1900s from an office high up in the Auditorium Building and I'll bet on hot summer evenings he used to go out on the roof and look around him. What was Louis Sullivan's vision? I think he envisioned a culture, not a high culture for the few but a patch of beauty for the many men and women who worked in this city and built it.

And what was in his mind's eye when he conceived the world's first skyscraper? He simply said, "It's tall." He saw more than steel and stone; he saw his creation reaching towards the heavens, aspiring. Louis Sullivan saw Chicago as more than a city of things; he saw it, as he put it himself, as a city of man.

Number One State Street, on the corner of Madison, was once known as the busiest corner in the world. The Carson Pirie Scott department store has been described as the jewel in Louis Sullivan's crown. It represents his vision of a department store that was more than a place of vulgar commerce. When a woman shops here, as women have done since before the turn of the century, she is surrounded by grace and beauty. The ironwork over the entrance reflects Sullivan's dream of a city that is more than a city of things, a city of men and women.

Wacker Drive

Opposite page
Carson Pirie Scott Department Store

The ethnic parade is as natural a part of Chicago as our river, which flows upstream. On any given Saturday, when the sun is shining and the weather is right, you will find a Polish parade, a Mexican parade, a Croatian parade, a Puerto Rican parade, a Ukrainian parade, a Black Bud Mulligan Day parade, or, of course, the most celebrated of all, the St. Patrick's Day parade.

Parades are often more than a display of pride: they are a not too subtle show of power. The Irish came here, after the Germans, escaping the potato famines in the old country, singing sad songs, and encountering signs that said "No Irish Need Apply". The Paddy had to work with pick and shovel to earn his daily bread and find his way upwards. Very often, to see the light, he entered politics. For almost a century, Chicago politics has been Irish. For the past forty years or so, our mayors have successively been named Kelly, Kennelly, Daley, and Byrne. Nowadays, new immigrants in the city, new people, have the same aspirations. The quest continues and so does the march.

Mike Royko is our most popular newspaper columnist and an observer of the human comedy that is "Chicaga", which is the Indian word for "wild onion". Royko has said, "Chicago's city motto is *urbs in horto*, meaning 'city in a garden'. I've been campaigning for years to have it changed to *ubi est mea*, which means 'Where's mine?'" The Chicago novelist Nelson Algren described this city as a city of "guys with dollar signs

for eyeballs", and it's still that way.
Everybody who came here, came
here to hustle a buck, anyway they
could get it.

The Chicago Water Tower is one of the few survivors of the great Chicago Fire of 1871, but not one of the showpieces of our town. When Oscar Wilde visited this city way back in 1882, he took one look at that and said, "What a castellated monstrosity, with small pepper pots stuck out all over it!" Ten years later, Rudyard Kipling saw Chicago and said, "Having seen this city, I urgently desire never to see it again. It is inhabited by savages and guttersnipes."

And Chicago is a city of working people, who came to earn their daily bread in heavy industries—steel, packing, railroads, farm equipment. They came seeking more than bread though. There has always been, in this city, this cockeyed wonder of a town, a quest for beauty.

But what would Oscar Wilde have said of Pablo Picasso's gift to Chicago? It came to our city about a hundred years after the Water Tower was built. The unveiling and dedication ceremony was on August 15, 1967. His Honour, Mayor Richard J. Daley himself, spoke of Chicago's Picasso, and the people were there in their hundreds to observe the statue —Picasso's Chicago, or Chicago's Picasso.

The Water Tower
Opposite page Picasso's *Chicago*

La Salle Station

In 1921 I was nine years old, arriving in Chicago for the first time, straw suitcase in hand, and stepping off the day coach at La Salle Station, one of the eight great railroad depots of this city. Between the years 1920 [and] 1930, three thousand trains stopped here ev[ery] day. You could not reach any American city [of] any size, transcontinentally, without stoppi[ng] off in Chicago. It was described as the railro[ad] centre of the world, and so it was. At the ag[e of] nine, I was just overwhelmed. I rode throug[h]

Chicago on the streetcar, three cents for a kid
at the time, and it was a big rough town where
so much was happening. Big Bill Thompson,
flamboyant, colourful, crooked, was the mayor,
and he said, "Throw away your hammer, pick
up your horn."

When I got off the streetcar, battered
luggage in my hand, I headed across to the
Wells Grand Hotel, the place my mother had
bought, near the north side of Chicago, where
it still stands today. Up the golden stairs the
men who lived there sat around in the lobby
and debated. They were skilled craftsmen,
self-educated men, boomer firemen, railroad
engineers, retired carpenters, cabinet makers,
and there was all sorts of discussion, fuelled by
a drop of whisky or two. Tom Paine, Jefferson,
Voltaire, Aristotle, wild, crazy, exhilarating talk
that left memories that still bless and burn my
mind.

Wells Grand Hotel

The black church is more than just a place to worship. It's a gathering of people who have worked hard all week and who on this day seek consolation, solace, and an airing of grievances, who seek a piece of that dream that seems so hard to find. Amazing grace exhilarates the spirit, makes a joyful noise unto the Lord and unto themselves. It says, "We are indeed somebody!"

The corner of 47th and Martin Luther King Jr. Drive was once called Grand Parkway, and then South Parkway. This space, this place, this boulevard was the Champs Elysées, 5th Avenue, Broadway all rolled into one for black Chicagoans. The Regal Theatre, as it used to be called, was the elegant place where, appropriately enough, Duke Ellington and Count Basie played, where Billie Holiday sang, and where Moms Mabley brought laughter.

On this corner you could meet, if you were black, someone from your hometown, everybody, anybody. On Saturday night, you were dressed in your Sunday best, but the one night I remember here on this corner was the time Joe Louis knocked out Max Schmeling in the first round. This was Liberation of Paris Day, Carnival Day, Emancipation Day, all at once. People walked five feet above the pavement; there was literally dancing in the streets; there was embraceable you; you were offered drinks and barbecue. It was glorious. Of course, that was 1937.

The old Regal Theater

From Eastern Europe, at the turn of the century and more recently, came the farmers, the peasants, the villagers, seeking that old familiar place. They found it in neighbourhoods among their own people. Many of these communities have vanished, drained by the flight to the surburbs, but stubbornly a good number have been maintained and kept going. A home away from home.

Chicago is a city of bungalows. On this street, throughout this neighbourhood, are these stucco-frame tidy little brick houses, and here live the sons and grandsons, daughters and granddaughters, of the people from the Old Country, the immigrants who came here seeking that better life. Often they have worked for the same company on the same job all their lives. To have these houses is that dream, a house of your own, a piece of land and, of course, a little bit of shrubbery; with the lawn well kept and manicured, preferably living among people of your own kind. On occasion suspicious of strangers, but more often than not showing a generosity of spirit, an open-heartedness, a sense of hospitality.

Chicago is no one-dimensional town, nor are its people. No, signora, Chicago is more than that, much much more. And so up Jacob's ladder, one more rung upward towards the blue heaven of security. That is to own a two-flat, your piece of land but you're a landlord as well. On the first floor you and your family live, and up above your son-in-law and his family, or even a stranger. So you're getting rent. But always, if possible, a patch of green, a little garden, a flower or two — that quietly desperate search for just a small piece of beauty in everyday life.

A mural in the street — we call it wall art in Chicago and it is found in every community in town. In the Chicano and Puerto Rican area, it is the work of young people living on the block. They did it themselves and they have probably never heard of Diego Rivera or of Orozco, but what they are telling us is, Behold our vision, our quest! We hear about vandalism in large cities all over the world and defacement of walls, but there is no record of any defacement of Chicago's wall art. The reason is quite simple: the young people's pride in their art and in themselves.

On Sunday morning, Maxwell Street becomes Chicago's open market. Years ago, the market used to

Maxwell Street

fill, block after block, mile after mile, with wall-to-wall people. Expressways have cut the heart out of the area, yet there is still life in these few old blocks. Here you can buy anything you want, whether it's a used bicycle tire, a hot wristwatch, or half a dozen bananas. *Chacun à son goût*, each to his own taste, buddy. And here you can hear the sounds of street singers and of hawkers unabashedly peddling their wares. This is no suburban supermarket. These are the few remaining small entrepreneurs at work, young Horatio Algers, offering anything you want. This is Maxwell Street, and the people haven't changed much here. There are more black people and Latinos today than there were in the past. But they are still people, whether they are new arrivals to Chicago or young couples who just want to pick up a bargain.

The "L"

Riding the "L" is the means of transportation to and from work for hundreds and thousands of Chicago people, five and sometimes six days a week. Downtown the elevated railroad forms a loop, and the Loop is Chicago's name for downtown. When somebody says, "I'm going down to the Loop", that means I'm going to where the action is, where the shopping is, where theatres are, where people walk — that's the Loop. It's about eight blocks north to south, about six blocks east to west. Almost square, you might say — the mathematician's dream, squaring the circle.

Walk through the Loop on a Saturday — that has always been the festive day, morning, noon, and at night, when you went to the movies. Today's young black people and young working-class white kids go to the Loop to see so-called exploitation movies such as *Kung-fu Mama*, *Malibu High*, *Malibu Low*. I remember June 1925, my graduation day from McLaren Public School, when I went down to the Loop in my first pair of long pants and saw Cecil B. De Mille's *The Ten Commandments*. Talk about exploitation of the Good Book!

For years now there has been talk of tearing down the Loop because of the noise of the trains. But if anything the high decibel level adds to the excitement of downtown; you know you're somewhere. There has been talk of tearing it down, much as there has been talk of tearing down the Water Tower, but both survive, two oldtime institutions of Chicago, two survivors.

The Loop

The evening shows Chicago as a city of motion, but even more as always a working city. In the centre it is mostly white-collar people, of course, coming out of offices. On the outskirts of town, you have the blue collars heading home. All seemingly going in opposite directions: some, the executives, going towards the northern suburbs; others, blue collars mostly, heading towards the west and south. No general rule, the multidimensional aspect of a city in motion.

To some, Chicago with its lack of sophistication and its muscularity is comical, archaic in this cool era, somewhat like an old punch-drunk fighter, swinging wild roundhouse wallops to the laughter of the wisenheimers at the ringside. But when it connects — oh, baby! As Nelson Algren put it, "In order to rap any sort of joint, you have to love it a little while, its alleys as well as its boulevards. . . . Chicago's rusty heart has room both for the hustler and the square. . . ." Algren speaks for me too. And so, if I were ever to meet that old signora in that northern Italian town again and she were to say to me, "Chicago, boom, boom, boom", I'd still say, "Oh, no, signora, no, no, Chicago is more than that, much more."

MAI ZETTERLING'S
Stockholm

MAI ZETTERLING'S
Stockholm

Taking a bird's-eye view over my city, what do
I see? A city that has been named city of light
and water, city of space and grace, city
between the bridges . . . city of my childhood.

There used to be a tradition in my country of introducing oneself with one's title. So allow me to introduce myself — author, actress, film-maker, Mai Zetterling. I am just a mortal human being with a civic registration number as proof that I exist. And when I die, my number will be put on another computer. This way I will never get lost.

There are many Stockholms and the name means many things to many people, but for me it is the city of a thousand trades, the city of silent crowds, the city with no faces, the city of no dreams, the city with a million hidden people, the city with the greatest solitude, the city of prosperity. The city with its hard liquor zone. Yes, we have problems with alcohol that are described as neurotic. The largest monopoly in the world is Sweden's System Bolaget, a state-run chain of stores for alcohol.

The city of dark winters and many gloomy months. You are sure to have a warm welcome when you arrive, but if you arrive in mid-winter don't be surprised if you are overcome by something we Stockholmers call Lapp-sickness. It is a kind of melancholy induced by too much darkness. Hence the upturned faces whenever the sun decides to shine, however briefly.

A long time ago Stockholm was described by a visiting monarch as "a Fair House and a Godly City". A golden city surrounded by frozen water leading to the Baltic, the city with red- and saffron-coloured houses, with at least one acre of park for every one hundred and fifty inhabitants. As recently as the middle of the nineteenth century, we were one of the poorest and most underdeveloped countries in Europe. Very soon, there will be two cars for every family unit. And it is the cheapest country for telephones in the world.

Modern Stockholm was born on the small island which is known popularly as "The City Between the Bridges". The old town is its heart: a jumble of narrow streets and cosy restaurants, small squares that accommodate some kind of commerce or other.

The word "stock" means "logs", which were connected with chains and thrown into the water to protect the island against invasion. "Holm" was the contemporary word for "island" — so it was "Stockholm".

A city official said not long ago that Stockholm was built in the wrong place. In the old times the rulers did not want to make it comfortable. They were thinking of military strategy, a place difficult to get at, and it certainly is that, guarded, as it is, by a great archipelago.

Gustav Vasa is supposed to have been Sweden's greatest ruler and he looked upon Stockholm as the nation's greatest fortress. He was considered the founder of modern Sweden, our George Washington.

A sixteenth-century traveller once called Stockholm "a trading village which thinks it is a city". That was true then, but now it is a boom town which thinks it is a village. Its population has almost tripled in only half a century. It is a young city, yet near the heart of the city the old village feeling has been kept and guarded. Every part of our country is represented here, every style — manor houses, peasant dwellings, churches, old inns. It is a well-known and well-loved part of Stockholm, and it is called Skansen. Stockholm's most

STOCKHOLM

famous writer, the tormented genius of the theatre, August Strindberg, used to come to Skansen for early-morning outings, to free his mind from the demons and the angels that seemed to leave him no peace.

The gloomy months of winter are the price that Stockholm has to pay for the brilliant glory of its summer, and the culmination comes on that very important day for a Swede, Midsummer, when there is singing and dancing all through the night in open spaces like Skansen, and a fair bit of drinking as well. At Midsummer you can read a newspaper at midnight without any artificial light. Nobody sleeps. The night is luminous with a light so intense that it must be seen to be believed.

Opposite page (top) Skansen

The National Theatre in Stockholm has been called the Star Factory. Greta Garbo and the two great Bergmans, Ingmar and Ingrid, emerged from it. It has a school with a three-year course in drama, so when I was young I took my courage in both hands and ventured into the monumental place. I used to sit on the steps with my eyes downcast and never thought that I really belonged there, but to my great surprise I was accepted at the age of eighteen and within a year was playing important roles in Shakespeare and, of course, in Strindberg.

Naturally, Strindberg had had a lot to say about acting and actresses: "The art of acting seems to be the easiest of all the arts. Any person can walk, talk, make gestures, but that is the person herself and that is not art. Give a person a role to play, however, and there the difficulties begin. The darling of the stage, that dear little woman, she knows she has a charming figure, lovely legs and a pair of flirtatious eyes. Being charming is all she knows and she uses it. It has certainly nothing to do with talent. If she has words to say, we usually cannot hear them and, if we do, there is no depth behind the words. And beware of our darling who knows she has a lovely voice. She only listens to herself and does not take into account what the author had to say. I should know — I was married to two charming darling actresses myself."

Poor old Strindberg — women, always women.

The National Theatre

Strindberg also seemed to suggest that
something was rotten in the state of Sweden:
"I don't think I am exaggerating when I
maintain that the Swedish nation is a stupid,
conceited, slavish, envious and uncouth
nation." Yet there is a Norwegian joke that
goes, "There is only one thing wrong with the
Swedes. They are perfect."

A Swede says, "Yes, look, look what a smart
place we Swedes have made for ourselves, look
how hard we work, and how well we look after
each other. We are so beautifully organized, so
clean. Everything is fine, just fine." Why then
the boredom? Why this middle-aged mood,
why is the rate of suicide still high, why has
mental illness risen? Can there be some grain of
truth in what the Norwegians say about us?

Stockholm is the city that provides commu-
ter tickets for dogs on trains and buses. It is
probably the most law-abiding town in Western
Europe, with laws and restrictions, reforms and
protections against almost everything. A city

with the architecture of seven centuries and in
at least seventeen styles. Its god is a silent
Lutheran God with little impact on society.
Efforts have been made to disestablish the
Lutheran Church. Most young people, indeed
most people, are negative or indifferent to
religion.

   This is the city which has been regarded by
the world as a model city, socially and
culturally. However, there is a system of
compulsory military service for men between
the ages of eighteen and forty-seven.
This is a city poised between East and West
that has the highest life expectancy in the
world. And the highest standard of living in
Europe. Everything is organized for its people,
except sleep.

Neutrality has been a keynote of our foreign policy. We have had no war since 1814. Our last prime minister had this to say on the subject: "All in all we live in an evil world. One sign of it is that we believe we have to have a military defence, that it is a must in the world we live in." And a minister said recently: "It is of course impossible to say how strong our defences must be." Hence Stockholm has built a large underground shelter as protection against nuclear attack. In peacetime it is used as a garage. If war comes, there are eleven pages at the back of the telephone directory that will tell you what to do: listen for alarm signals, put on the radio, draw the curtains, find a safe place, and take with you some warm clothes, a sleeping bag, food and drink for two days, identity cards, et cetera. Odd that one of the best prepared countries in Europe should be the most neutral.

But this city is prepared for practically everything. Keep the city controlled, keep the traffic flowing, keep the city clean, trust no man, safety first. Again, so they say, we are better prepared than most cities in Europe as regards overall control of a city. Drunkenness is a problem; so are narcotics, so is traffic, and so indeed is boredom. The police are demanding more control and they will certainly get it. They emphasize that it is necessary.

Leonardo da Vinci once wrote: "He who possesses most is also most afraid of loss." We have won gold medals for our safety locks, have won prizes throughout Europe for our double treble locks. We are certainly a consumer society. We have been called a gadget society. And there have been discussions of which kind of society people really want.

What do the Swedish people want for the coming year — do you know? Some money in the bank, a pleasant evening at home with friends, children they can be proud of. Perhaps I have been away from Stockholm too long, as I do not seem to have the same kind of wishes as my compatriots. Here are my wishes then — inner growth, insecurity, love.

JOHN HUSTON'S
Dublin

JOHN HUSTON'S
Dublin

Opposite page   The River Liffey

Long ago, just a little upstream from what is now the centre of Dublin, there was a ford across the River Liffey that gave Dublin its earliest name — Baile Atha Cliath, meaning in Gaelic, "the town of the ford of hurdles". As the town grew it assumed its present name of Dublin, Gaelic for "dark pool". About a thousand years ago, the ships of the Viking invaders were anchored along the quays of the river, and the town they built spread itself up the slopes.

The span upstream from O'Connell Bridge is a mere youngster of the nineteenth century. It was once a toll footbridge, and the poet and Nobel Prize winner W.B. Yeats used to tell that when he was a student he was too poor to afford the toll charge of one halfpenny and had to go all the way round by O'Connell Bridge to get across the river. The tollkeeper at the time used to make a joke of it, and Dubliners still call it the "Halfpenny Bridge".

It is something of a habit with Dubliners to make a joke of poverty and misfortune. It is a way of showing their familiarity with both. Whatever his original racial origins, which could be Gaelic or Norman, Danish or English or Norse, the average Dubliner views life with a mixture of wry humour and a sort of serene fatalism. Perhaps it is due to the history of his native city — a long history of siege, pestilence, invasion, rebellion, slaughter, persecution, and civil war. Whatever the cause, he tends to believe that the worst is inevitable and must be endured.

The most traumatic chapter of Dublin's history centred around the General Post Office on O'Connell Street, where bullet holes in the angels around the statue of Daniel O'Connell, an earlier Irish patriot, still bear witness to the Rising of 1916. At Easter that year, a few hundred insurgents against British rule took over the Post Office and declared Ireland to be a republic. It was the one successful act of defiance in a history of failures that went back over seven hundred years. The insurgents held out for a week. Eventually, with the Post Office and most of O'Connell Street on fire from the shelling of a gunboat in the Liffey, they were forced to surrender.

One by one, the leaders were sentenced to death by military courts and shot. Dubliners, apathetic and even antagonistic at first, were shocked into pity and anger. With the executions in Kilmainham Jail, what ought to have been the end of a puny drama blazed into four years of street ambushes and guerrilla raids. Pearse, one of the insurgent leaders, was a poet — indeed, many of them were poets. It is sometimes called the Poets' Revolution.

"And the sins of the fathers shall be visited". . . . In September 1916, when the executions had finished and the city was plunged into grief, W.B. Yeats set out the mood of Ireland in the much-quoted lament:

. . . And what if excess of love
Bewildered them till they died?
I write it out in a verse —
MacDonagh and MacBride
And Connolly and Pearse
Now and in time to be,
Wherever green is worn,
Are changed, changed utterly:
A terrible beauty is born.

The tragic plight of the north of Ireland today cannot be reckoned without counting the misdeeds of the English in Dublin in 1916.

General Post Office

Kilmainham Jail

The strange thing about Dublin, so predominantly Catholic a city, is that it has two ancient Protestant cathedrals but no proper Catholic one.

According to legend, St. Patrick's Cathedral stands on the spot where, in the fifth century, St. Patrick miraculously created a well of pure water when the citizens complained to him that the water they were compelled to drink was marshy and evil-tasting. Within is laid the body of Jonathan Swift, "Doctor of Divinity. Dean of this Cathedral Church. Where fierce indignation can no longer lacerate the heart. Go, traveller, and imitate if you can this earnest and dedicated champion of Liberty."

He died on October 19, 1745, aged seventy-eight years, and had been born just a stone's throw away in 1667. When he returned from England to take up the position of dean, he declared it his ambition to enjoy the serene, peaceful state of being a fool among knaves. Instead, he has been remembered as being the benefactor of Dublin's poor and the champion of papist and Protestant alike in the battle to preserve the modest liberties of the citizens.

Above Swift's resting place hang the now ragged colours of Irish regiments, reminders that the rank and file of Queen Victoria's army was largely Irish Catholic and its officers Anglo-Irish Protestant. They carved out Victoria's empire and fought on through the First and Second World Wars. Winston Churchill pointed out that there were more Irish per capita in the British army than there were English.

Opposite page St. Patrick's Cathedral

My introduction to Ireland was when I was
invited for a week during the Dublin Horse
Show. My first night was at a hunt ball at the
Gresham Hotel. I forget what hunt it was, but
in the course of the evening things got wilder
and wilder. It was quite a night. I had a
marvellous time. Afterwards we took the cars
and headed off to a country house in the hills
nearby. It was all dark and we went down a
precipitous road—a sense of trees and racing
clouds and mists. When I awoke in the
morning, I went to the window—and there was
a black lake, and a granite mountain with the
heather over it like a shawl over a piano. And I
belonged to Ireland.

Horse racing and hound racing are something of a religion in Ireland. I think it is remarkable that at the races in Ireland the crowd knows more about racing than anywhere else in the world. The old ladies are handicappers; they know what the weights should be, and when they figure a race it will probably run very close to form.

The Irishman loves his horse. It is almost the symbol of Ireland. The Irish hunt and show their horses with enormous pride, and Ireland is the breeding place of the bone that furnishes the great brood mares of the world. They come from Ireland and, for a few generations, they are bred in California, Kentucky, Arabia, Germany—everywhere. Eventually they begin to thin out, and breeders have to come back to Ireland for more brood mares. In any case, thanks to the great Irish turf, the horses will go on and on forever.

Horse racing has been called the sport of kings; dog racing is for everybody. A greyhound is not hard to keep, and many a fan has his hopes of sudden wealth in a kennel in his back garden. "Let's go to the dogs", the slogan says, and huge Dublin crowds flock to Shelbourne and Harold's Cross parks every night of the week.

The Brazen Head Hotel is the oldest tavern in the city and one of its earlier patrons was the martyred patriot, Robert Emmet—bold Robert Emmet, the darling of Erin, who went to the English gallows with a smile: "Farewell, companions, I'm going to leave you. I lay down my life for the young who will die."

Some of the city's finest entertainment is still performed at the Brazen Head. In Dublin, music and laughter get on very well together in pubs devoted to both. Back at the beginning of the eighteenth century, Turlough Carolan, the most celebrated of Irish tavern harpers, took to the bottle. When his friends advised him to sober up, he said, "He who would give up drink is a foolish person." And many a Dubliner would agree with him. The late Brendan Behan, for instance.

Behan was a disputatious figure in life. Many of his polite literary encounters ended in knock-down, drag-out fights. In my opinion, he was baited into much of that simply to make copy for the press. Nevertheless, Brendan was not all that popular with a lot of Irishmen. They thought he projected a false image—the brawling Irish drunk. I knew Brendan well,

and I swear that if they had only let him sing,
all would have been tranquil. But the bad
memories are fading and only the best of him is
remembered. Brendan has been elevated into
the hierarchy of poets — than which, excepting
saints, there is no higher in Dublin.

   Patrick Kavanagh was another poet and
well-known character in the life of the city.
Brendan Behan and he were literary enemies.
A seat beside the canal is his memorial and
some of his poetry is inscribed on a stone
nearby:

O commemorate me where there is water,
Canal water preferably, so stilly
Greeny at the heart of summer. Brother
Commemorate me thus beautifully. . . .
O commemorate me with no hero-courageous
Tomb — just a canal-bank seat for the passer-by.

Antiquity broods here in Dublin, emanating
from a fragment of wall, a flight of steps,
remains of the tenth-century Norse city.

Dublin has a legacy from its past of
subjugation and persecution, a brooding wist-
fulness which seems to linger still in the
grey-faced buildings and in the procession of
bridges across its river. But it has retained
many noble and valuable things, too, especially
its eighteenth-century buildings.

According to chroniclers, in the grimmer
reigns of Henry VIII, Elizabeth, and James I the
gates of Dublin Castle were sometimes
garnished with the grinning skulls of executed
Irish chieftains. Until 1920 the castle remained
the seat of British rule in Ireland, although the
custom of festooning the gateway with skulls
was quietly dropped.

Its grand interior has in seven centuries been the setting of levées and balls, of presentations of débutantes to the reigning viceroys, and of all the intrigues, triumphs, and betrayals that go along with privilege and pomp. The throne dates from the time of William of Orange and he himself may have presented it to the castle. George V was the last English monarch to sit on it, and now any Irish citizen, and I am one, may do so if he has the nerve.

Dublin Castle

Old age and ruthless development have taken their toll of Georgian Dublin. Nevertheless what remains enshrines the aristocratic lifestyle of the period, and its committed concern for architectural elegance. In the following centuries, when the elegance had become a little worn, the great figures of the Irish literary revival lived in the noble streets or walked and talked their way along them — George Moore, W.B. Yeats, Lady Gregory, George Russell, J.M. Synge, James Joyce, Oliver St. John Gogarty, to name but a few of a brilliant company of writers and wits.

That was the fashionable Dublin. But there was another side, where the decline and decay of the once gracious houses was matched by the poverty and deprivation of those crammed into them, often ten to a room — Dublin's poor. At the time of the Easter Rising and the subsequent War of Independence, these people were suffering the highest death rate in Europe from hunger and ill health. Sean O'Casey was one of their kind, and when he became a dramatist he peopled the stage of the Abbey Theatre with them — the braggart men and the heroic long-suffering women.

Trinity College was founded in 1591, at the wish of Queen Elizabeth, for the avowed purpose of converting the Catholic Irish to the Protestant religion. It succeeded instead in turning out some of Ireland's most distinguished rebels and at least one generation of students who, when asked to toast King William of Orange, drank instead to the health of a horse that had thrown him. But its list of luminaries is long and includes men like Oliver Goldsmith, Thomas Moore, Edmund Burke, and Bishop Berkeley, the philosopher who held that "the world must vanish instantly if God ceased for one moment to be aware of it".

Trinity College

James Joyce walked along Dublin's strand on a
June day in 1904. He looked around at the
lighthouse perched there on the end of the
causeway, at the hill on the further side of the
bay, then at the houses bordering the shore and
the mountains rising behind them. "If I close
my eyes," he wondered, "would it all be there
still when I open them again?" So he closed his
eyes and then he opened them. "And yes, all
was there still, gold light on sea, on sand, on
boulders. The sea is there, the slender trees,
the lemon houses." Later he put it all down in
a book called *Ulysses* and gave Dublin its place
as a centre of literature.

The martello tower at Sandycove is only one
of several similar forts along the Dublin
coastline. Joyce lived there for a time with
Oliver St. John Gogarty. Later the tower came
to figure in the opening pages of *Ulysses*, where
Joyce lampooned Gogarty under the name of
Buck Mulligan. "Stately plump Buck Mulligan

came from the stairhead bearing a bowl of lather on which a mirror and a razor lay crossed. A yellow dressing-gown, ungirdled, was sustained gently behind him by the mild morning air. He held the bowl aloft and intoned: '*Introibo ad altare Dei*'. . . . He faced about and blessed gravely thrice the tower, the surrounding country and the awakening mountains."

"Shall we sit down together for a while," Denis Johnston, the Irish playwright, once wrote, "here where we can look upon the city, strumpet city, in the sunset, so old, so sick with memories, old mother? You, I know, will walk the streets of Paradise, head high, and unashamed."

Martello tower

ANTHONY BURGESS'
Rome

ANTHONY BURGESS'
Rome

Rome is the city that was not built in a day.
Neither can it be seen in one short chapter of a
book. Unless, that is, you see it with somebody
like me. I am not a guide; I am not a tourist. I
am merely an aging British writer who came to
Rome to write.

But why not write somewhere else? In Manchester, England, where I was born, or London, or Toronto? The answer is, I think, that in many of our great industrial cities, writing, making poetry, music, statues, or churches is not really approved of. It is not part of the day's work. The day's work is making bread and mending shoes and building machines.

In Rome, however, art is part of daily life. One makes one's statues or poems or books as one makes bread or mends shoes. Art is part of Rome's business. And Rome itself is a work of art as well as a living, breathing being, which is what all cities should be.

When I was a young Catholic living in Manchester, the priests used to tell me that Rome was my mother. But others have told me (and these include some of the ancient Roman poets) that Rome is a whore. Perhaps the two, mother and whore, are not really incompatible; perhaps they are not what most men seek in a woman, the very reason why they should not seek them in a city. Rome is a mother. Rome is a whore. Rome can be domineering, imperious, corrupt, vicious. But Rome can never be ungenerous. Rome gives all of her sensual pleasures, without stint.

At roof-top level, Rome may seem a city of spires and steeples and towers that reach up towards eternal truths. But the city is not built in the sky. It is built on dirt, earth, dung, copulation, death, humanity. It is also built on a river, which the Romans call the Tevere.

On one bank of the Tevere is the city of Rome proper; on the other bank is the district of Trastevere

(meaning "across the Tevere") whose
people, the Trasteverini, regard
themselves as the true Romans.
When you read Shakespeare's *Julius
Caesar* and he describes a Roman mob
with sweaty nightcaps, stinking of
garlic, then you know he's referring to
the Trasteverini.

Trastevere is the district where I
lived and worked, and its people are
self-sufficient, totally different from
the posh Romans living along the Via
Veneto. I lived for a long time on the
same busy square, and I would
probably still be living there if the
landlord had not thrown me out. I
wrote a lot of books there. It is a noisy
square, but I rather liked the noise; it
was a sign that life was going on
outside. It was not solely the noise of
Lambrettas and theatres; it was the
noise of men at work, men making
fake antique furniture or genuine
bedsteads. I thought that I was part of
the activity and that my work was
somehow as useful as theirs. I used to
wander about that square among the
parked cars, looking for the right
words and sometimes finding them.
When I felt more than usually
depressed, I would look up at the
ornamental putti or cherubim above
the great doorway and take pleasure
in the fact that two of them seemed to
be making the Communist salute.
Very Roman.

Trastevere

Top   Belli statue
Bottom   Casa Dante

Giuseppe Gioacchino Belli guards one of the entrances to the Trastevere. He was schizophrenic, in a sense. As a Vatican official, he was a censor of theatrical presentations. But in his spare time he wrote 2,275 sonnets in the Romanesque language of the streets. He created a voice for the common people — common people who had always been downtrodden, by popes as well as by bureaucrats. It is ironic that near Belli's statue stands the Casa Dante, the house where the great poet Dante stayed when he came from Florence; ironic, because Dante created the language which we are told is good Italian, *dolce*, full of honey and high thoughts. But the language of the Trasteverini is rough, scurrilous, blasphemous, obscene, the tongue of the gutter. Many of them are leaders of intensity, rebels against the government. They have had two thousand years of bad government and they must look forward to two thousand more. As they say, "*Il combattimento continua*" — "The struggle continues."

The Colosseum, for most of us, stands as the great, broken symbol of Rome's pagan power, and we always associate paganism with cruelty. We have been misled a little by Hollywood into thinking that the sole purpose of this Colosseum was to torture Christians and feed them to the lions. In fact, most of the torturing and mutilation and killing of Christians was done in Nero's circus, which no longer stands; St. Peter's now occupies its former site. In nineteenth-century poetry and fiction, the Colosseum became a highly romantic place, not associated with cruelty at all; Victorian heroines used to walk there by moonlight with their cavalieri and sometimes died of Roman fever. We can remember, if we like, that not only Christians suffered here, but Jews also. The Jews were not actually fed to the lions, but

Colosseum

they were used in building the huge structure, and many of them died in the process. When the Romans were subsisting on corn doles and wine and tribute from all parts of their vast empire, what they really looked forward to most was the show at the Colosseum.

It was only in the last century, at the beginning of the Romantic movement, that people began to admire and coddle ancient classical ruins. But during the Dark and Middle Ages and the Renaissance, during the days of Michelangelo, when people wanted marble as material for building and sculpture, they knew where to find it. The ruins of classical Rome were really a quarry. One early example of a structure that was preyed upon for its marble is the Theatre of Marcellus. It was built by the Emperor Augustus in memory of his beloved nephew, Marcellus, and Romans were supposed to come and see plays here. But the Romans did not like plays very much. They have never liked them, unless the play involved copulation on the stage, with real-life mutilation and execution by unwilling actors who were condemned criminals. Romans much prefer to have their cruelty, their bloodshed, and their mutilation undiluted by words.

At a point where the River Tevere runs wide, there stands a bridge called the Ponte Milvio. About seventeen hundred years ago, 313 A.D. to be exact, a battle was fought on this bridge. All over the Roman Empire at that time, the Goths, the Vandals, the Germanic hordes were breaking in — even as far away as the remote province of Britain. But here the battle was fierce. As the Emperor Constantine stood on this bridge, he looked up in the sky and saw a fiery cross, and he heard a voice saying, "*In hoc signo vinces*" — "In this sign you will conquer". Constantine did conquer, but from that time onwards the Roman Empire was a Christian empire. The coming of a new religion to a nation is never a sudden revolutionary act. Christianity had been known, of course, in Rome, but the Christians had been regarded as outcasts, mere meat for lions in the Colosseum. They were heretics: they did not worship the emperor; therefore they had to be persecuted. But now the downtrodden religion became the religion of the rulers themselves. And it all began on this bridge.

Above (left)   The Theatre of Marcellus
Above (right)   The Ponte Milvio

Piazza San Pietro, St. Peter's Square, is the site of the most glorious and most extravagant Christian monument in the world, the Basilica of St. Peter, symbol of the papal power that Garibaldi and his fellow republicans were fighting in the nineteenth century. This is the seat of the leader of the world's Catholics, and yet it seems to denote secular rather than spiritual power.

St. Peter's Square

The trouble with Rome, you see, is that it does not help you to think of higher things; it is too much a city of stone and mortar and water and wine and life. And the Basilica itself stands as a symbol of the papacy's desire to be remembered in this world rather than to reap its reward in the next.

Garibaldi memorial

Despite the traditions, Rome is not in fact a
holy city. The Romans are not a holy people;
they are pagans. Indeed, a priest in Rome is
regarded as a sort of weird animal, not quite
man, not quite woman, and I have seen people
make the sign against the evil eye in the
presence of a priest. Romans are anti-clerical:
they do not like priests, and they do not like
popes. What they have against the pope, I
think, is not his power as a spiritual leader, but

The wall of the Vatican

the long tradition which made the papacy the temporal power in this city.

At the beginning of the last century, the citizens of Rome had been ruled by the pope for so long that they began to feel there might be better things in the world than papal despotism. And in 1849, the issue was fought out on a hill above the city. The pope's own soldiers, the papal zouaves, with the assistance of the French, fought the Republican patriots led by Giuseppe Garibaldi, and the papal forces lost. A memorial to Garibaldi and the Romans who died supporting him still stands on the spot.

The wall of the Vatican resembles the wall of a prison—understandably, since the Vatican is now quite separate from Rome, although it is in Rome and is totally Roman. It is the smallest kingdom in the world, with its own banks, monetary system, post office, and radio station.

The great English poet, John Keats, died in a
house at the foot of the Spanish Steps, on
Piazza di Spagna. He could look down from his
window on the steps, but in his day the crowds
there were not tourists. Many of them were
artists' models, because the area has always
been a centre of art and writing, but most of all
of painting. Like many a young English
consumptive of the time, he had come to Rome
in the hope that the mild air of the city would
cure his condition, but it did not. He died in
February 1821, the same year as Napoleon
died, although Napoleon was twice Keats's
age. This was the end of an era; the Romantic
period was coming to a close.

Keats could go to sleep listening to the
watery music of a nearby fountain by Bernini.
But nobody can hear that music now above the
roar of Roman traffic.

In the middle of the Piazza Navona stands
the big statuesque fountain that Bernini made
three hundred years ago. It represents the four
main rivers of the world, and it is very Roman
in its baroque style, pushing things to the limit,
making stone behave like human flesh, like
drapery, palm fronds, or even like water. It is
typical of the spirit of Rome in that it glories in
extravagance, but the glory never becomes
magniloquent or arrogant. There is always the
saving quality of wit.

See how one of the statues raises a hand
against the Church of St. Agnese, built by
Bernini's great rival, Borromini. The hand
seems to indicate that the place is going to fall
over. It has not fallen over in the last three
hundred years, and it never will.

The Spanish Steps

Top Piazza Navona
Bottom Bernini fountain

"The Wedding Cake"

The Unknown Soldier of Italy is buried within
the huge structure of the Vittorio Emanuele
monument, which is sometimes called the
"Wedding Cake". It is a long way in feeling
and spirit from the art of the nearby
Campidoglio, but it is not the lowest point to
which Roman public architecture can sink.
Mussolini Dux — Mussolini the Leader — the
rigid geometry of this obelisk, erected in the
tenth year of Il Duce's reign, excludes
everything that is round and irregular and
essentially human. And nearby are some
further examples of fascist architecture, a
glorification of the future heroes whom the
regime would make fit and strong: you are
welcome to them.

Above   Fascist statues in the Foro Italico
Left   Mussolini obelisk

Temple of Minerva

The Borghese Gardens—my gardens really because Burgess is Borghese in Italian. Of course, the humble Burgess family could never compare with that great Roman one into which Pauline Bonaparte married to become a Principessa Borghese. Imagine her, if you like, walking in these private grounds. But because those days are over and great men with great tracts of land no longer exist in Rome, the gardens now belong to the people. Visitors to Rome are always a bit disturbed when they come here seeking nature in the raw and find themselves confronted by the inevitable Roman busts. But the busts of artists, musicians, and writers serve a purpose: they remind us that the city is not far away and that we must be ready to plunge once more into the world where people create things.

Pagan Rome and Christian Rome are somehow combined in compromise. The Baths of Diocletian became a church; the Temple of Minerva became a shrine to the Virgin Mary. In the Campidoglio can be found an ancient statue of the goddess Minerva. Nearby stands a church called Santa Maria Sopra Minerva, Holy Mary on top of Minerva; the Virgin's shrine has been raised on the ruins of the temple of a pagan goddess. The two elements, the pagan and the Christian, are crowned by a third, the human touch of art and architecture which draws all the elements together.

Top Borghese Gardens

Rome is what a city should be, a place for human beings, not for machines. A place not too great, not too overbearing, where man can realize his best potentiality, be himself.

What is really surprising about this city is its continuity of culture. The life, the way of living, the way of thinking persist and nothing is thrown away; things are just added, and added again. Probably Rome has changed less in two thousand years than Manhattan has in twenty years.

As to the future, the poet Giuseppe Belli seemed to think that Rome would always be here, or at least until the Day of Judgement, a Day of Judgement that would somehow be a typically Roman event. The final words spoken, as the universal dark descends, will not be *gute nacht*, or *bonsoir*, or good night, but *buona sera*....

MELINA MERCOURI'S
Athens

MELINA MERCOURI'S
Athens

Athens is like a great mother who opens her heart to Greeks from every part of the country. Even though she has already stretched beyond what is physically bearable, in her heart Athens always has room for one more Greek.

There's a saying that two watermelons don't fit under the same arm; but Athens, which only sixty years ago had four hundred thousand people, embraces nearly four million today. Many were farmers. The soil was not always rich, governments were often neglectful, and school facilities were meagre. So they came to Athens in hope of a better life. The city has been a magnet for all those who were starving, physically and spiritually: Athens has better schools, theatres, and entertainment, as well as better job opportunities.

Very few can claim to be as true an Athenian as I am. The first man I loved was called Spiros. He was extremely handsome, extremely seductive. He was strong, he was tall, and he loved the people of Athens. He loved his wife and cheated on her. He loved his sons and took care of them. And he had a passion for me. It made my childhood very happy.

Spiros was my grandfather. He was also Mayor of Athens for thirty years, and there is a street in the city named after him, Spiros Mercouri.

I became a deputy of the Socialist Party in the Greek parliament in November 1977. For me it was a triumph, winning my first election, a moment of great emotion, especially since I received fifty-one per cent of my votes from women. I believe that the people of Piraeus are honouring my struggle against the dictatorship of the Junta, not Melina Mercouri the actress. I am committed to these people and I will never abandon them. I want to fight for them, in parliament, in the press, on the street, and I shall always feel proud, as I do now, when they come to me with their problems as old friends, calling me warmly "Melina", and never "Miss Mercouri".

And whenever I return to the port area of Piraeus, because it was here we filmed *Never on Sunday*, I feel a bit like Ulysses when he returned to Ithaca. Whether or not there is someone on the dock waiting for me with a bouquet of roses, I feel tenderness for the place, a sense of security. This is where I belong.

Piraeus

The Parthenon

They say that Athens was named after the goddess Athena, who cast her spear into the holy rock of the Acropolis and made an olive tree — the tree that symbolizes peace and productivity — sprout from it. But others claim that the word "Athens" comes from the Homeric *esēkōthē*, which means "I have climbed". So, Athens is the city on a hill.

We call the Acropolis the Holy Rock. The Parthenon has stood on it for two and a half thousand years, resisting time; its dazzling beauty has given the world proof of the glory of Greek civilization. It belonged to Athens, but

of course now it belongs to the whole world,
and the people of the world flood to it, to see it,
to touch it.

I am not one of those who cherish the past so
much that they forget the present. But when I
come up here on the Acropolis, I am embraced
by the past. Here, there is a sense of balance
and beauty, and this harmonious marriage of art
and nature exhilarates me.

What I love most in the world is Greece and
the Greek people. To be born Greek is to be
magnificently cursed. To a surprisingly large
number of people, it means that you personally
built the Acropolis, you created Delphi and its
theatre, and you gave birth to the concept of
democracy. But the truth is that you are poor,
many of your people cannot read, and the rare
moments in which you tasted of democracy and
independence were often snatched away from
you by foreign protectors and their Greek
puppets.

In the shade of the Acropolis is the district of
Monastiraki, a place that breathes, yells, and
sells everything imaginable. Here the rich and
the poor meet, all looking for bargains. And
what happens is classic. Foreign tourists are
persuaded to buy a *kompoloï*, often called
"worry beads", and immediately they feel a
little Greek. As for the Greeks, they want an
American windbreaker or a pair of jeans or a
second-hand Japanese camera. The language
of commerce is universal, but it is more
persuasive in Greek.

Oh, the Greek language, how well it suits
me! It has taught me so many lovely words:
pallekari — "my brave one", *thalassa* — "sea",
ouranos — "sky", *matia mou* — "my eyes",
agape mou — "my love". No wonder that within
sixteen years, two Nobel prizes have been
awarded to Greek poets — to George Seferis
and to Odysseus Elytis — and Lenin Prizes to
two other Greek poets — Varnales and Ritsos.

Monastiraki

When I was in exile, I felt a great nostalgia for Greece. I became so obsessed with all things Greek that people started calling me a professional Greek. I did not mind at all. All things Greek move me. When I am away, the Greek national anthem can make me cry.

On October 28, 1940, Hitler's partner Mussolini attacked Greece and demanded surrender. The answer was *ochi*, the Greek word for "no". The first victory over the Fascists occurred when the Greek army and the Greek people drove them out of Greece. Ever since, Ochi Day has been celebrated as a national holiday. But sadly, the authorities consider only those who share their political opinions have the right to commemorate the occasion. The police obeyed their orders, but they haven't stopped me from speaking.

Here, in my own constituency, we have come full circle. The very men of the Junta who deprived me of my citizenship and declared me a non-Greek lie behind prison walls. When they denounced me, I said, "I was born Greek, I shall die Greek!" But those bastards, they were born Fascists, they will die Fascists. That dictatorship has left many wounds in the Greek people, and I hope they will remain behind those walls all their lives.

Ochi Day services

A dictatorship is a humiliation for Greek people, a humiliation for the Greek soul. I am not one of those people who forget, and I hope that the Greeks will never forget that humiliation. The first cemetery of Athens is very beautiful. I dream of being buried here, with my grandfather and my father. And here, too, is the much-admired *Sleeping Beauty*, by the great sculptor, Chalepas, who is also buried here. And so is Alekos Panagoulēs, a resistance hero during the dictatorship, who was willing to risk his life to kill the dictator Papadopoulos. For six years he resisted the most atrocious tortures. Afterwards he died in a most curious car accident.

ΣΟΦΙΑ Κ. ΑΦΕΝΤΑΚΗ
ΕΤΩΝ 18 ΑΠΕΒΙΩΣΕΝ 17 ΔΕΚΕΜΒΡΙΟΥ 1873

Chalepas' *Sleeping Beauty*

And my mother's grave is here. She was beautiful when she was young, and marvello[us] company to me. I will never forget her. She died in Athens in 1972 when I was in exile, forbidden to set foot in Greece. I heard of he[r] death from my husband who was then in Ne[w] York. I was in Italy. The terrible news crush[ed] me. I told my husband and my brother that I must go to Athens. Both of them had been accused of terrorism by the Junta, and had al[so] been forbidden to enter Greece.

In defiance of the Junta, the three of us we[nt] to Athens. The dictators were afraid that if w[e] were arrested at the airport and not allowed t[o] attend the funeral, there would be world-wid[e] publicity against them. We were allowed to enter the city, but only for six hours.

Those were the years when Greeks would
use any opportunity, especially a funeral, to
express their opposition to the tyrants. Some
two hundred people, mostly people of the
theatre and the arts and politicians released
from jail, came to that private affair. And, of
course, there were many informers and police
as well, about two hundred of them.

The press photographers were eager for me
to shed some tears, but I wouldn't cry. I didn't
want the Colonels of the Junta to see my
suffering.   Panagoulēs' grave

Monastery of Kaisariani

The monastery of Kaisariani in the hills above Athens is holy. Not only because it was a place of worship, but because many brave Greeks died near here. The earth is sacred, drenched with the blood of hundreds of brave young men who gave their lives fighting against Fascism and Nazism.

On May 1, 1944, two hundred of those young men were executed. They were not the first nor the last. Among them was Spēlios Ampelogiannēs, a twenty-year-old who found time before he was shot to write a note. He pinned it to his jacket and threw it out into the street. The message said: "This is how honourable Greeks die — proud. Long live freedom. Passer-by, please take this coat to the above address. It is the last wish of a man who knew how to die."

It was the students of Athens who, in November 1973, barricaded themselves in the Polytechnic and, after a thirty-six-hour battle with the tanks of the Junta, helped to bring about liberty. It is worth noting that in Greece there is no actual generation gap, because the children and their parents have struggled for the same things.

To end this journey through Athens,
I have a story to tell. A hundred and
sixty years ago, the Turks were on the
Acropolis, besieged by the Greeks.
They ran out of lead for their bullets
and began destroying the ancient
columns of the Parthenon in order to
use the metal that runs through the
centre of them. The Greeks saw what
was happening and sent a message to
the Turks, asking them to stop

destroying the columns: "If you need lead, we will send you some."

And the Greeks did. That is how much our ancestors loved this city and its treasures. And I love it too. But I don't see only the ruins, I also see an eternally beating heart. A heart that beats stronger today than ever before.

I love this city. For a while I had to be away from it. But I hope never to be again. Athens may break your heart at times. But no other city has the power to move me to tears and laughter at the same time.

This is my city, and this is where I will stay forever. I belong here. You understand, my friends?